Anthropological Papers

Museum of Anthropology, University of Michigan
No. 80

Living in a Lean-to
Philippine Negrito Foragers in Transition

by
Navin K. Rai

with a foreword by Karl L. Hutterer

Ann Arbor
1990

© 1990 by The Regents of the University of Michigan

All rights reserved

ISBN 978-0-915703-17-3 (paper)

ISBN 978-1-949098-92-1 (ebook)

Cover design by Marty Somberg

Library of Congress Cataloging-in-Publication Data
Rai, Navin K.
    Living in a lean-to : Philippine Negrito foragers in transition /by Navin K. Rai ; with a foreword by Karl L. Hutterer.
      p. cm. — (Anthropological papers / Museum of Anthropology, University of Michigan ; no. 80)
    Bibliography: p.
    ISBN 0-915703-17-3
    1. Aeta (Philippine people) 2. Aeta (Philippine people)—Social conditions. 3. Social change—Philippines—Case studies. I. Title. II. Series: Anthropological papers (University of Michigan. Museum of Anthropology) ; no. 80.
GN2.M5   no. 80
[DS666.A3]
306 s—dc20
[306'.0899911]
                                                    89-12557
                                                       CIP

To Mana, Shiru, and Xitu

Contents

Maps, Figures and Plates, *vii*
List of Appendices, *vii*
Foreword, *ix*
Preface, *xiii*
Note on Orthography, *xv*

PART I. INTRODUCTION

    1. The People, *3*
    2. The Perspective, *11*
    3. The Setting, *17*

PART II. THE TRADITIONAL WORLD

    4. The Natural Environment, *25*
    5. The Social Groupings, *31*
    6. The Forest Orientation, *45*
    7. The Social Circumscription, *61*

PART III. THE TRANSITIONAL WORLD

    8. The Changes, *73*
    9. The Economic Transition, *85*
    10. The Consequences, *97*

PART IV. CONCLUSIONS

    11. Summary, *113*
    12. The Agta Future, *121*

Chapter Notes, *127*
References Cited, *129*
Plates, *153*
Appendices, *175*

Maps, Figures and Plates

MAP 1. Eastern part of the province of Isabela, *8*
MAP 2. Homeland areas of the Agta linguistic groups in Isabela, *65*

FIGURE 1. Diagram of Agta kin categories, *33*
FIGURE 2. Chart showing residence choices of Disabungan Agta women, *42*

PLATES

1. Agta by the Diwago River, *155*
2. Fishing camp on the Malibu River, *157*
3. Fishing camp on the Malibu River, *159*
4. Agta dry season houses, *161*
5. Spearfishing in the Malibu River, *163*
6. Caryota palm processing, *165*
7. Man and children, *167*
8. Agta family leaving on hunting trip, *169*
9. Unmarried man, *171*
10. Unmarried woman, *173*

APPENDICES

APPENDIX 1. Population distribution of Agta in Isabela by municipality, *175*
APPENDIX 2. Population distribution of Agta in Isabela by socioresidential unit, *176*
APPENDIX 3. Shared basic vocabulary of northeastern Luzon languages, *177*
APPENDIX 4. Terms of reference among the Disabungan Agta, *178*
APPENDIX 5. Work/non-work ratios among a band of Disabungan Agta, *179*
APPENDIX 6. Work activity schedule, *180*
APPENDIX 7. Hunting activity analysis, *181*
APPENDIX 8. Agta adult height and weight figures, *182*
APPENDIX 9. Food energy conversion table, *182*
APPENDIX 10. Caloric contribution of activities, *183*
APPENDIX 11. Nutritional intake of a band of Disabungan Agta, *183*
APPENDIX 12. Energy expenditure of a band of Disabungan Agta, *184*

Foreword

by Karl L. Hutterer
Museum of Anthropology, University of Michigan

More than 200 years ago, Spanish reports referring to *"negritos"*—short, dark-skinned people living in the Philippine forests—described them as a primitive race, doomed to imminent extinction. A hundred years later, when American soldiers and administrators accommodated themselves in the islands, they sounded the same theme. The notions of cultural backwardness were wrong, and the announcements of demise premature. Now, however, as we near the end of the twentieth century, Negrito societies are indeed involved in a desparate struggle for survival, a threat to their existence that stems from economic and political actions that flow directly from long-standing and deep-seated notions of social inferiority. These are the realities that frame Navin Rai's study.

Although curiosity about Philippine Negrito cultures was always intense, no detailed or comprehensive information about them was collected during the 350 years of Spanish rule, and few professional studies were carried out in the first sixty years of this century. Fieldwork among hunter-gatherers in the tropical forest is burdensome and difficult, a fact Rai alludes to briefly and self-effacingly in his introductory chapter. Only recently has the detailed and conceptually focused information begun to be assembled that is the basis of all sound social and cultural research, demanding long-term, sustained fieldwork and close association between researchers and host communitites. Rai's work is one of four or five such intensive recent studies of Philippine Negritos, all focused on groups living in the rugged Cordilleran region of northwestern Luzon (others are by J. Peterson, P. Bion Griffin and A. Estioko-Griffin, P. Bennagen, and T. Headland).

The seminal 1966 conference on hunting and gathering peoples and the publication in 1968 of the conference proceedings under the title *Man the Hunter* stimulated a resurgence of anthropological interest in such societies. This conference was directed at developing possible models for the social and cultural organizations of hominid and human populations in early prehistory, and in the context of the rise of a broad-based popular as well as scientific interest in ecology, at a more general effort to understand ecological relationships characteristic of small-scale societies with relatively simple organization. It was believed that this might help in developing basic principles of human ecology, eventually applicable to more complex situtations with social systems of a greater scope.

Much of the early research effort following the *Man the Hunter* impetus centered on hunter-gatherers in arid areas, with work carried out in southern Africa being particularly influential. Involving years of often very systematic and detailed observation, this early research produced a wealth of startling data and a long series of interpretations that continuously forced revisions of previous conceptions. This work yielded many ecological insights of broad general interest, ranging from the interplay between environment, subsistence technology and settlement pattern to the impact of dietary and behavioral variables on fertility. However it also demonstrated far greater complexity in social as well as ecological relations than many had expected, and pointed out both short-term and long-term dynamics in the existence of these populations that, under the influence of our naive Western prejudices, we had not previously been willing to attribute to these societies. What had begun as an effort to build models for the life and organization of the earliest men and women turned into a revelation that portrayed the contemporary hunter-gatherers of arid South Africa as peoples with tangible histories, the latest chapter of which concerns their role in the complex political life of the South African region.

Contemporary hunger-gatherers are, of course, not only found in the arid regions of Africa and Australia, but also in the Arctic as well as in the tropical forests of South America, central Africa, and Southeast Asia. Just as a "Bushman model" was threatening to dominate anthropological and popular perceptions of hunting and collecting peoples, a second wave of researchers began to fan out into the rain forests, generating new insights into the diversity of hunting and gathering organizations. Dr. Rai's work is part of this second phase of post-*Man the Hunter* research, and some of its importance must be seen in this context. It contributes to a slowly growing body of ever more detailed and sophisticated information about foragers in humid tropical habitats. Based on the foundations laid by the work in South Africa, these more recent research efforts have developed their own distinctive set of problem foci, conceptual approaches, and methodologies. Important concerns cluster around defining the nature of the resource base constituted by a tropical rain forest; the constraints it imposes on the organization of human communities; interactions and interdependencies between hunting and nonhunting populations; and so forth.

Dr. Rai's study makes important contributions to these discussions and it should be seen in this context. Beyond it, however, it is also a significant addition to our ethnographic knowledge and understanding of a Philippine people. Between the facts and figures, the Agta emerge as a people with a history that, albeit still poorly known, makes their present struggle particularly poignant. There are suggestions that their ancestors have been in contact with agricultural populations for hundreds of years, that they have traded with them for a long time, and that their own marginal agricultural involvement is of some antiquity. It all adds up to a picture of a dynamic people who have seen slow but constant change throughout their existence, a people who have made an art of living in a difficult and unpredictable environment, making accommodations to both nature and neighbors. Yet, while suggestions of slow but long-term social and economic change make the notion of "pure" hunter-gatherers a romantic fiction of little value, recent intrusions on Agta life propelled by national and international economic and political forces are confronting them with the need for changes so rapid and drastic that their social and biological existence is literally threatened. As large timber companies cut the forest in huge swaths, land-starved agricultural populations arrive in the wake of the loggers to claim the cleared land for fields. While few today would explicitly subscribe to the nineteenth-century notions of primitiveness and inferiority ascribed to hunters and gatherers like the Agta, the contemporary political economy is still based on these assumptions, thus permitting, and perhaps even demanding, their disenfranchisement. For the Agta, the irrevocable loss of forest habitat resembles the simultaneous loss of both home and job for the urbanite.

Dr. Rai weaves together a rich account that includes careful ethnography, ecological analysis, historical perspective, and sincere concern for the well-being of the subjects of his study under the current conditions of accelerated ecological change. His sensitivity is perhaps accentuated by the fact that this research is one of only a few examples of Asian anthropologists studying societies outside their own homelands. It constitutes a step toward replacing the dominance of Western anthropologists in the field, a step toward the decolonization of our discipline. The end of this long road will be reached when scholars like Dr. Rai come to America and Europe to study communities in our midst.

Preface

This book documents the ethnography and change among a group of tropical rain forest hunter-gatherers, the Agta of northeastern Luzon, Philippines. The Agta represent one of the few surviving foraging societies in Asia. While they are considered the most traditional hunter-gatherers of the Philippine Negritos, they have, at the same time, experienced changes in the last two centuries.

The book is derived from my doctoral dissertation (The University of Hawaii, 1982), which was based upon field research conducted in 1979 and 1980, but with two main revisions. First, some theoretical discussions have been condensed. Second, while no new field data were incorporated, some new findings from recent studies of the Philippine Negritos in general, and the Agta in particular, are discussed.

Looking at the Agta from the systems perspective, this study attempts a holistic description of the Agta society, and a systematic description of its change. I have also tried to incorporate and explain the indigenous Agta viewpoint, whenever possible, because it is crucial to the understanding and scientific explanation of the social processes of the Agta.

Agta foragers, unlike most other rain forest foragers, are primarily hunters, and rely secondarily on gathering and fishing. I say they are primarily hunters because, in addition to making an impressive caloric contribution to their diet, and requiring a high investment of time and energy, hunting provides the basis for the Agta socio-symbolic identity.

In recent centuries, the Agta forest home has been heavily encroached upon by outside agricultural and mercantile population; the resulting interactions have precipitated a multitude of changes for the Agta, including a dependence on the nontraditional economic strategies of external trade, horticulture, and wage labor. The fragile transition state of the Agta, today characterized by a non-forest orientation, stands in sharp contrast to their past conditions and leaves them in a predicament. The continuing environmental degradation of their homeland leaves the Agta with no option except to emphasize the nonforaging way of life, but their subjugation by outsiders, as well as the inherent socioeconomic incompatibilities, makes this shift a difficult one.

While the particular aim of the present work is to document the change among the Agta due to a dramatically altered condition, it should also serve as a general descriptive model of change among other contemporary hunting and gathering societies.

This study has benefited in innumerable ways from the support of many people. I would like to extend my sincere gratitude to my teacher and friend, Bion Griffin, of the University of Hawaii, who initiated me into Agta studies and contributed both his time and knowledge to the completion of my doctoral dissertation. I am also deeply grateful to my teachers Jack Bilmes, Alice Dewey, Richard Lieban, Brian Murton, and Alan Howard. I must also duly acknowledge the inspiration and moral support given to me by Karl Hutterer, of the University of Michigan, to revise and edit this dissertation into a monograph. The final revision of the manuscript benefited from discussions with John D. Speth, also of the University of Michigan, and to whom I am grateful.

A number of institutions graciously supported this study. In particular, the Centre for Nepal and Asian Studies, Kathmandu, granted my long leave of absence to complete the study. The East-West Culture and Communication Institute, Honolulu, provided grants to carry out the field research, and the Center for Asian and Pacific Studies, Honolulu, to complete the dissertation-writing. The monograph was revised and edited while I was a visiting Fulbright Scholar with the Center for South and Southeast Asian Studies, University of Michigan, Ann Arbor.

In the Philippines, I was extended unconditional research affiliations from three institutions: the National Museum, the Philippine Center for Advanced Studies, and the Philippine Psychology Research and Training House. Among Filipino individuals, I owe deep gratitude to Virgilio Enriquez, Gloria Chan, Professor Ponciano Bennagen, Abe Padilla, and the Estioko family for their camraderie. From the field research area, I am grateful to Carlos Dumelod, mayor of San Mariano Municipality, for providing enduring friendship to boost my occasionally eroding morale during fieldwork.

Most of all, my deepest acknowledgment is to the Agta of Isabela, who without fully understanding my reasons or purposes in living among them, patiently allowed me to "mind their business." At times, my foreign ways must have made their lives difficult, but I recall only the tender moments of my stay with them. Excluding the errors, which are entirely and always mine, I share this work with them all.

I must also acknowledge the help of a number of my colleagues, in particular, James F. Fisher, Pete Brosius, Thomas Headland, Agnes Estioko-Griffin, and Shirley Mayfield for their academic support in the writing and revision of this work. I acknowledge the kindness of Bion Griffin and Agnes Estioko-Griffin for allowing me to publish their Agta photographs. Finally I express my deep gratitude to Sally Horvath for painstakingly editing the manuscript for publication, to Kay Clahassey for cartographic and photographic assistance, and to Gail Teachout for secretarial support.

Navin Rai
Kathmandu, 1989

Note on Orthography

Vernacular words of the Disabungen Agta dialect are written in italics unless the context suggests such treatment unnecessary. Following the orthography developed by Headland and Headland (1974:xii–xxvii), Agta words are written phonemically, except for the velar nasal, which is symbolized as *ng*, and the mid-close central vowel (often called the Austronesian "pepet" vowel), which is written *é*. Glottal stops, which are predictable before initial vowels and after final vowels of utterances, and between certain vowel sequences, are not indicated. Words in non-Agta languages are also italicized with the particular language identified by an intitial: *I* for Ilokano, *T* for Tagalog, and *K* for Kalinga.

PART I

INTRODUCTION

1
The People

The Agta Negritos of the Philippines are among the few surviving groups of tropical rain forest foragers. Scarcer still are foragers who, like the Agta, derive most of their subsistence from hunting, rather than from gathering or fishing. It is, therefore, no coincidence that among the Philippine Negritos, the Agta are a prime target of study by anthropologists. Time seems to be finally catching up with the Agta, however, and in the last few decades they have experienced dramatic changes in their traditional way of life. This study is an attempt to describe both the traditional life of the Agta before it disappears, and to document the changes that have occurred so far.

Hunter-Gatherers

In anthropological literature, hunting and gathering populations such as the Agta Negritos are continually referred to as examples of "primitive" human societies. This blanket term needs qualification if it is to be used at all. To laypeople, the word "primitive" often suggests that these societies are somehow lower down on the evolutionary ladder—the surviving remnants of a less enlightened era. Far from being an imperfectly evolved mode of subsistence, however, the hunting and gathering adaptation has been persistently successful, a fact firmly substantiated by archaeological studies of prehistoric peoples. Ecologically speaking, a hunting and gathering way of life is merely a strategy to exploit a different niche than that of the so-called "civilized" societies. While hunter-gatherers may possess a technology that is primitive, they may represent the opposite scale, in say, religion.

Even to trained social scientists the word "primitive" can be misleading. It might seem to suggest that hunter-gatherers lead simple, one-dimensional lives, when, in fact, hunter-gatherers do not embrace one single mode of subsistence, but several, often interwoven in complex ways. There are hunter-gatherers who have a more traditional, forest-oriented way of life. Others are semi-sedentary food-collectors and fishers whose economy is structurally very similar to that of an agricultural population. Then there are those contemporary hunter-gatherers who base their economy on trade of local products with outsiders, and cash hunters whose trade is tied to national and international market economies. These economic variations of the hunter-gatherers are paralleled by their equally diverse social organizations.

Hunter-gatherer societies are those in which primary reliance is on hunting, gathering and fishing. They generally derive their sustenance from a broad spectrum of resources (Flannery 1971:55–56), and depend on simple manipulation rather than complex transformation of the natural environment (Harris 1977:14). Hunter-gatherers are energetically simple people, who use mostly human energy, or very small amounts of other energy sources. Socioculturally they tend to be nomadic and egalitarian.

Prehistory tells us that change has characterized the hunting and gathering way of life since the Pleistocene. While this way of life is rapidly disappearing today, the large-scale transformation of hunting and gathering cultures has not yet received its due attention (Lee and DeVore 1968). Considering that much anthropological theory-building is based on studies of modern hunter-gatherers, more analytical studies are needed. And, considering that the number of living hunter-gatherers is shrinking at a rapid rate (Lee 1978:1), their study has special urgency.

The transformation of hunting and gathering societies today seems to exemplify the most dramatic case of change among human societies in at least two respects. First, the hunting and gathering way of life today, if only an adaptation to a different niche, is still radically dissimilar from that of agriculturalists. The transformation of prehistoric hunter-gatherers into Neolithic agriculturalists has been called a "revolution" (Childe 1961). The contemporary shifts from hunting and gathering to agricultural or industrial adaptations can mean an equally radical departure. Second, hunter-gatherers have lived in relatively isolated frontiers. During the historical period, outsiders encroached on the hunter-gatherer homelands to exploit various resources on a scale that has no precedent. This "frontier process," as J. H. Bodley has called it (1975:24), has generally been insurmountable.

The Agta Negritos

Continental, peninsular and insular Asia contained numerous hunting and gathering groups until the early decades of this century. There was a great deal of enthusiasm for research on these groups, particularly during the colonial era of Asian history. While other groups also attracted attention, the most notable studies were conducted among the various groups of Negritos (in Spanish, "small black people") of South and Southeast Asia (e.g., Man 1883; Radcliffe-Brown 1932; Schebesta 1927, 1952–57). The end of the colonial period marked the decline in studies of hunter-gatherers in Asia. The Asian hunter-gatherers as a whole are thus a little-studied group today, and consequently, there is a paucity of ethnographic data on these groups.

The accelerated intervention by outsiders at the turn of this century affected hunter-gatherers worldwide (Lee et al. 1968:5), and the Asian hunter-gatherers were no exception. The general ethnographic literature pertaining to technologically simple societies of Asia indicates that their way of life has been changing, particularly since the early decades of this century.

The implementation of externally initiated "planned" change among Asian hunter-gatherers also began in the 1930s. Governments, colonial or otherwise, sponsored resettlement projects for these generally nomadic people and, in most cases, vigorously campaigned against the continuation of a hunting and gathering way of life (Harrison 1949; Sinha 1972; Carey 1976). The government programs were mostly rooted in what Bodley calls technological ethnocentrism (1975:10). Describing the hunting and gathering way of life as "wild" and thus inferior, the government assumed that the only way for these people to become "civilized" was for them to settle down. In tropical and subtropical areas, hunter-gatherers were also expected to become agriculturalists. The increasing trends of settlement permanence and the agricultural way of life were viewed as positive developments for these technologically "primitive" people. This unfortunately lingering ethnocentric assumption is the basis for the continued effort of governments to introduce planned change among hunter-gatherers. One such group that experienced the continued pressure for planned change was the Philippine Negritos.

The Philippine Negritos[1] have always fascinated missionaries, travelers and colonial administrators; consequently, they have perhaps one of the longest historical records of Asian hunter-gatherers. There are, however, only three intensive ethnographic studies on the Philippine Negrito groups in the pre-World War II literature: Reed 1904, Vanoverbergh 1937–38, and Garvan 1963 (written during the pre-World War II period). At the end of World War II, some more specialized studies describing the Negrito culture and subsistence pattern began to appear, for example Fox 1953.

The Philippine Negritos are found widely scattered through all three major island chains: the Luzon, Bisayan and Mindanao. The ethnogenesis of the group is still being debated. One hypothesis, called the Wave Theory, claims that when successive waves of human immigration in prehistoric times populated the Philippines, the Negritos were one of the earliest people to enter the islands (Kroeber 1928:54). This hypothesis, however, has remained unproven due to lack of archaeological evidence (Fox 1972:3). On the basis of their phenotypic characteristics and a few religious practices, the Negritos of the Philippines have always been placed in a category along with other Asian Negritos: the Andaman Islanders and the Semang of Malaysia (Cooper 1940; Schebesta 1952–57; Maceda 1964). However, recently Solheim has suggested that these different groups of Asian Negritos "evolved locally under similar lowland rain forest ecological conditions" (1981:25; see also Rambo 1988). Human geneticists are also finding that even within the Philippine Negritos, the groups do not show similar genetic markers (Omoto 1981:421; 1985). These findings suggest that the Negrito groups have had different origins and immigration histories and have remained semi-isolated human breeding populations (Pascacio et al. 1974:224).

While we assume that the Philippine Negritos were relatively isolated hunter-gatherers centuries ago (Eder 1987:12), their economic exchange with the neighboring agricultural and horticultural populations is not new. Spanish records claim that barter trade between these groups existed at least as early as the seventeenth century (see Headland 1986:211–13 for details). The Negritos were also employed by neighboring populations as woodcutters and agricultural wage laborers. They were occasionally taken as household slaves as recently as the 1920s (Larkin 1972:5; see also Worcester 1913). Strained relationships between the Negritos and their neighbors sometimes resulted in inter-ethnic raids. In some areas, the Negritos prohibited the lowlanders from cutting timber, hunting in the forest or fishing in the river, without paying "tribute" for such access (Rahmann 1963:144–51).

Today, the Philippine Negritos have become increasingly interdependent with outside agricultural populations. As a result of increased interactions with outsiders, their traditional economic independence has been terminated. More recently, mercantile activities such as logging and mining have catastrophically altered the Negrito environment and promoted immigration of outside populations into the Negrito homeland. Many Negrito groups have been forced to farm to counterbalance their declining wild food resources.

Fox (1953:173) had earlier on urged the search for some common cultural and linguistic elements peculiar to the scattered Negrito groups to help define basic elements of an earlier Negrito culture. However, linguistic research has shown that there is no common linguistic element that is shared among the Negrito groups which is distinct from other Philippine ethnic groups. Further, some Negrito languages share fewer cognates with each other than they do with non-Negrito languages of the area (Headland 1981a:12). Despite decades-long anthropological research among groups of Philippine Negritos, no substantive detail of wider, pan-Negrito applicability has been discovered, except for their traditional foraging adaptation.

Changes in the sociocultural elements of the various Negrito groups is, on the other hand, one common phenomenon. While this adaptive process among the Philippine Negritos in general has been the topic of numerous studies (Maceda 1964; Cadelina 1982; Eder 1987), this study attempts to look at this change more closely among the Negritos of northeastern Luzon.

The Negritos living in northeastern Luzon call themselves Agta. The Agta are the most traditional group of the Philippine Negritos and represent one of the few surviving hunter-gatherer societies in Asia. Technologically simple, the Agta have for millennia derived their sustenance from daily foraging of wild resources. Except for a little trade with the neighboring settlers, and occasional, rudimentary swiddening practices, the Agta were invariably left to themselves in their rather impenetrable forest home.

The Agta Negritos today speak various languages of the Austronesian subfamily called Northern Cordilleran (Tharp 1974:107). Linguists suggest that the Negrito groups such as the Agta originally spoke languages which were not Austronesian. Sometime, around the middle of the second millennium B.C., they adopted languages of their Austronesian-speaking neighbors (Headland and Reid 1989:46–47; see also Vanoverbergh 1937:9–10). As with other Philippine minority groups, the Agta languages share cognates with the neighboring and regional languages.

The Agta have experienced changes throughout prehistoric and historic times due mainly to the contact with and encroachments of the outside populations. It is assumed that the Negrito groups like the Agta represent one of the oldest human strata among populations of the island of Luzon (see Keesing 1962:334, 361). As populations from other Philippine islands or other parts of Southeast Asia immigrated, the Agta were forced to concentrate in enclaves. During the colonial era of the Philippine history, the Agta homeland shrank further as immigrants who fled the colonial rule penetrated the area. At this time, the Spanish and American colonial administrators directly influenced the Agta as they tried to rehabilitate Agta "at a civilized form of rule" (see Turnbull 1930). The Agta homeland was used as bases by various guerilla groups fighting the Spanish, American and Japanese rules (Griffin 1985a:88). Mercantile operations in this century brought encroachment on the Agta forest homeland and encouraged further immigration of outside populations. Today, while the guerilla New Peoples' Army controls a large section of Agta homeland, the current Philippine government continues to plan and implement programs to resettle the Agta.

There are two reasons to study change among the Agta of northeastern Luzon. First, the Agta exist in a unique situation. They have experienced contact and isolation from the outside population in varying degrees, group by group. Depending on the history of contact and encroachment by the outside population, the Agta groups show variations in their subsistence pattern. Thus, the Agta exhibit a socioeconomic continuum that reflects Philippine Negrito groups as a whole. Second, the body of ethnographic literature on the various groups of Agta is sufficient to allow the systematic analysis of change. For example, Bennagen (1976) provides a detailed ethnography of one particular group, the Palanan Agta (see Map 1). The traditional hunting and gathering practice of various groups of eastern Luzon Agta, including the southeastern Cagayan Agta, is documented (Estioko-Griffin and Griffin 1981; Griffin 1984; Estioko-Griffin 1984). An intensive

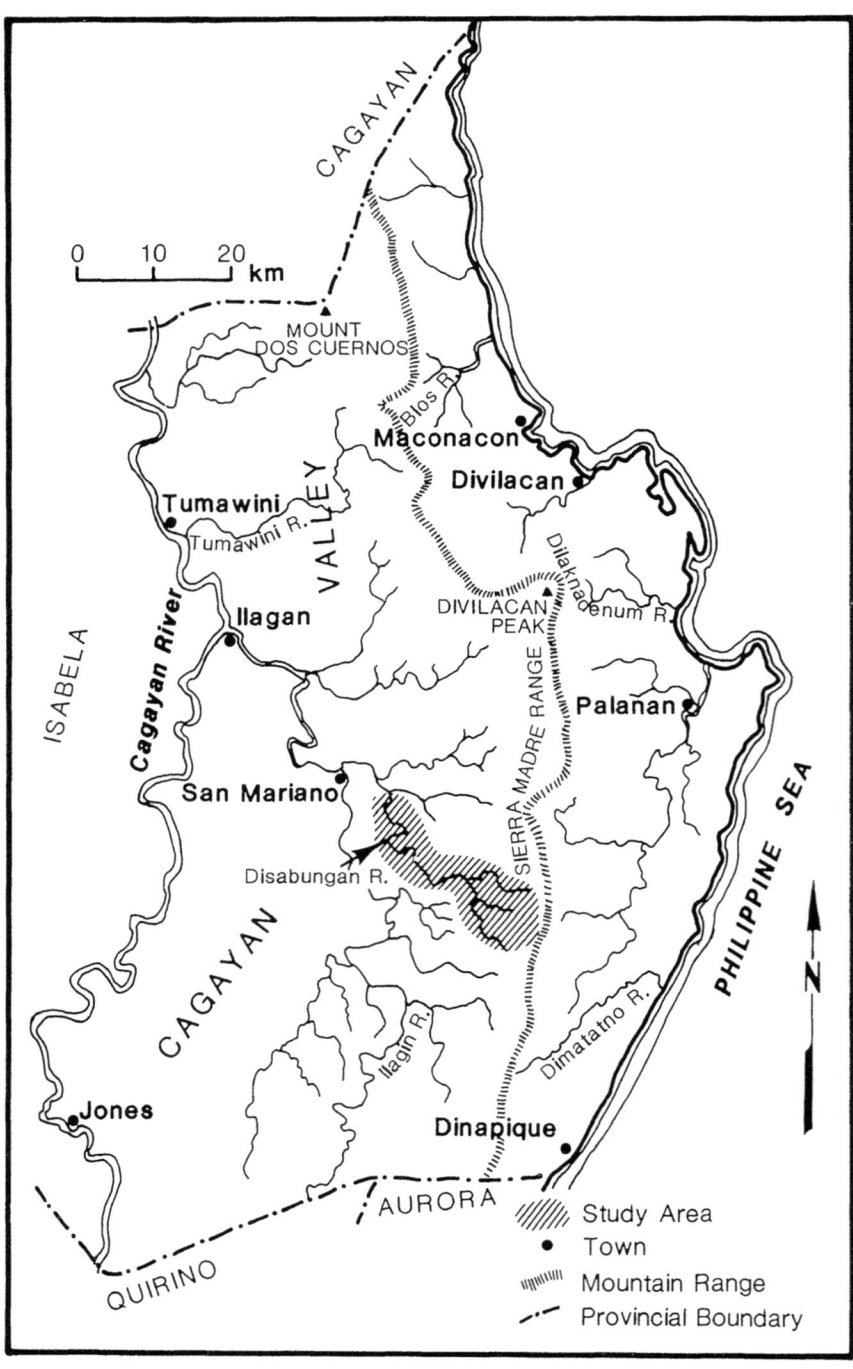

MAP 1. Eastern part of the province of Isabela.

The People

analysis on the nature of interaction between semi-settled Palanan Agta and their agricultural neighbors has been conducted (Peterson 1978a, 1981, 1984). A further analysis of the Agta-lowlander exchange and the demographic consequences among the Casiguran Agta has also been completed (Headland 1986). Additional data on various aspects of Agta ethnography and their environment are available (Goodman et al. 1985; Allen 1985; Mudar 1985; Simon 1982; Barbosa 1988; Clark 1986; see also Simangan 1956; Zipangang 1970; Pili 1979). Linguistic studies of various groups of Agta have also been documented (Headland and Headland 1974; Nickell 1985; see also Vanoverbergh 1937–38).

2
The Perspective

Anthropologists ask three basic questions in their study of change among human societies. First, why does a human society change (Steward 1955:5)? Second, how does change in a human society take place (Barth 1967:661; Flannery 1972:6)? Third, what does change mean to a human society experiencing it? These three questions represent aspects of the analysis of change, called the conditions, the processes, and the consequences, and comprise the main foci of anthropological studies of change.

Theoretical Perspective

Anthropological studies since the 1960s have used a systems framework to analyze change among human societies (Flannery 1968; Rappaport 1968; Jochim 1979). The present study also borrows the general notion of systems to describe the conditions, processes, and consequences of change among the Agta society.

Anthropologists have long recognized that a culture is an organized system. For example, it was Durkheim (1965 [1895]) who made the explicit statement that any given aspect of a society is related directly or indirectly to all other aspects. The structural and functional schools of anthropology further elaborated the idea that changes in any institution by necessity lead to changes in other parts of the social system (Firth 1936; Evans-Pritchard 1940).

From the systems perspective, a human society is a complex living system (von Bertalanffy 1968:18). According to this perspective, a holistic analysis is needed to describe a human society adequately; all things have connections with many other things and the significance of any one depends on its relationship with others (von Bertalanffy 1968:38, 54). For the study of change among the Agta, a multitude of aspects of Agta society should be considered. However, a total description of the Agta society is, at least objectively speaking, not possible. Thus, the components and subcomponents most relevant to the study of change among the Agta will be described. There will be little direct analysis of linguistic and political aspects of Agta society, but aspects of the Agta society such as the ecosystem, settlement pattern, technology and social organization will receive more intensive attention.

Maruyama has suggested that a system tends to preserve or maintain its given form, organization, and state, by a process of *morphostasis*. At the same time, the system also undergoes a process of *morphogenesis* whereby it tends to elaborate or change the given form, structure, and state of the system (1963:164). Analysis of both the morphostatic and morphogenetic aspects of a human society is required to understand the change in that society. In this study, I will first describe the Agta traditional system to emphasize its morphostatic process. I will show that the Agta continue to maintain their traditional state through a mechanism of checks and balances applied to their ecosystem, settlement pattern and social organization. This will be followed by an analysis of the morphogenetic aspect of the Agta system. I will argue that alterations in the pre-existing demographic, ecological, and economic situations have resulted in the transformation of Agta society.

A society can be described differently depending upon whether the perspective of the observer or the perspective of the people studied is taken. The first, the *observer's model*, is an analytic one, in which the observer's perceptions are shaped from Western science. The second, the *insider's model*, on the other hand, is based on the categories and relations created by the people being studied. These two models are constructed here by applying the two perspectives originally suggested by Pike (1966, 1967).

The observer's model is constructed by using the *etic* approach, which attempts a relatively culture-free description of the society. Because the observer uses a descriptive notation derived from comparative study, the etic approach is an important step toward the construction of a model that will have cross-cultural application. Anthropologists have relied heavily on this approach to describe human societies. The *emic* approach is used to construct the insider's model. This approach attempts to construct a group's model of itself. It describes the group and its environment solely from the point of view of the subjects (Hardesty 1977:290). While anthropologists were always aware of it (e.g., Malinowski 1922:25), the emic approach was formalized by a relatively recent movement in social science called ethnoscience. Both the etic and emic approaches are used here to achieve the greatest possible analytic depth.

The state of society changes both because of the way people behave and in spite of how they behave. One of the characteristics of humans is to have some degree of cognitive anticipation (Bennett 1976b:848). The anticipation of people about their future conditions will affect their behavior and to some extent determine the course of events in the future. The conditions, processes and consequences of change are definitely related to the actual characteristics of the situation, but at the same time, they are also invariably related to how people themselves appraise and respond to the situation. In my discussion of various topics throughout this work, I will describe the Agta from the investigator's point of view and follow this with an attempt to present the description from the participant's perspective.

Field Methods

Fieldwork among the Agta Negritos was conducted between June, 1979, and May, 1980. The first month was spent in a preliminary survey of the field research area. The following six months were spent among the Disabungan Agta of San Mariano Muncipality, Isabela. The remaining months were divided among other Isabela and southeast Cagayan Agta groups. Prior to the fieldwork, I studied the trade language of northern Luzon, Ilokano. During the field research, I used my knowledge of Ilokano to learn the Agta language.

Studying a mobile hunting and gathering society like the Agta, one faces a different set of methodological problems than one faces studying a settled agricultural group. For example, as the Agta live in open lean-tos, one can constantly observe the ongoing activities in an Agta camp without having to visit their residences. However, often there are less than ten adults in an Agta band. To have interviewed them all the time would have soon tired them.

Added to this are the problems associated with incomplete control of the language. In my case, the interview technique was employed effectively only as my knowledge of the Agta language improved. Such sessions were deliberately kept unstructured and informants were given the flexibility to choose the direction of the conversation. Roughly once a week, interviews were conducted in a somewhat structured manner to verify the data collected through indirect observations. Even if the informal interviewing began with one single adult, it often became a group session. Women and children often volunteered to correct the male informants.

Participant observation was another important technique used in the data collection. Living among these foraging Agta bands, an anthropologist cannot remain marginal. As I was expected to take part in many of the day-to-day activities, participant observation became a normal routine. Some activities, like hunting, which required both energy and skill, were less frequently participated in, and therefore, less observed than others.

My typical day in the Agta camp began very early in the morning. As people woke up, I would inquire about their plans for the day. After breakfast, men usually left for the jungle for hunting or fishing. Women also often left for short foraging trips. If I did not join any such activities, I was left behind with the children in the camp. By lunch time, women and some men returned to cook and feed their children. A few would leave again for other foraging activity to return only by early evening.

Evenings were almost always colorful in the Agta camp. While either male or female members cooked, the remaining crowd converged on the hunt of the day or the consumer goods brought back from nearby agricultural settlements. Discussions ranged from game to camp movements. After the evening meal, the Agta retired to their family lean-tos. While the talk continued across lean-tos, some sang songs until late at night. Nights were usually quiet. During the colder nights, however, individuals would get up periodically to restart their fires. Sometimes dogs fought for space with humans and with other dogs, occasionally causing a lean-to to collapse over sleeping Agta family members.

My single greatest logistical problem in the field was related to the frequent camp movement of the Agta. It seriously limited the amount of outside food and other research supplies I could have. Obtaining supplies from the town and the neighboring barrio also became a problem, as I could not anticipate camp movements early enough to determine our locations. The problem became more serious during the northeast monsoon floods, when we were sometimes stranded for days.

In the camp itself, I had some problems. When the Agta break camp and the band splits into two groups, I had to decide which to accompany. The Agta make these decisions on the basis of their kinship network. Since I had none, I would arbitrarily decide to join one or the other group. Such random affiliation brought into question my "loyalty" to particular groups. In the early period of my fieldwork, there were subtle accusations that I was partial to whichever group I chose to travel with.

Collection of data pertaining to the Agta ethnohistory presented the most difficult methodological problem. Reconstruction of a society's distant past with the use of ethnographic techniques is always a difficult, if not risky, endeavour. Moreover, in the case of the Agta, this problem was aggravated as they do not seem to have a tradition of myths and folk tales. To make the best of the situation, I interviewed senior Agta informants to recollect the Agta past as they were told by their parents and grandparents. They were asked specifically as to their beliefs regarding their various subsistence strategies, foraging or otherwise; their technology complex; and their contact with the neighboring agricultural population. This information, supplemented by the available archaeological, linguistic and historical descriptions of the Agta area, is used here to reconstruct the Agta traditional world.

The Agta do not know their absolute age and sometimes not even their place of birth. To them, personal names represent the soul or the spirit of the bearer. They thus observe numerous name avoidances. For example, naming of the dead is conspicuously avoided by spouses, children, and even parents of the dead "because his spirit troubles the living." They also do not name certain categories of relatives. They hesitate to name parents "because they feel shy" and do not name an infant "because he gets woken up." One must not call names of close affines for "it causes boils" (*busale*). Understandably, Agta do not remember the names of dead relatives or the siblings, spouses, etc., of such dead relatives, beyond two to three generations. Serial monogamy, which is very common among the Agta, created complications as it was frequently underreported. Thus, the collection of genealogies required work with, and verification from, many informants.

For comparative purposes, a variety of Agta populations inhabiting the province of Isabela have been included in this study. This was done to insure that groups who represent different degrees in the socioeconomic continuum of the Agta be included. In order to handle the ethnographic information of this regional population in a less clumsy way, I have quantified the data as much as possible. Also, whenever it was possible and desirable, I attempted to quantify the data according to emic categories.

3
The Setting

The Disabungan Agta, who are the focus of the present study, live in the western (or valley) watershed of the Sierra Madre range in northeastern Luzon. According to the Philippine political-administrative divisions, the Disabungan Agta live within the municipality of San Mariano, in the province of Isabela (see Map 1).

Geographical Orientation

The northeastern Luzon region is geographically divided into two areas: the western Cagayan Valley and the eastern Sierra Madre range. Drained by the Cagayan River, the Cagayan Valley is a longitudinal basin of approximately 7,000 km^2. It is mainly composed of alluvial plain suitable for permanent agriculture. The Sierra Madre range, which runs north-south and extends to southeastern Luzon, is 30 to 60 km in width and is primarily forest.

The province of Isabela comprises the central part of the Cagayan Valley as well as one central section of the Sierra Madre range. With a land area of 10,761 km^2, the province is made up of valley plains, undulating hills, mountains and coastal areas. In 1977, the population of Isabela, excluding the Agta Negritos, was estimated to be 766,000, the majority of whom were concentrated in the eastern valley plains (PDA 1978:16–18).

The province of Isabela experiences a mean monthly temperature of 25° Celsius. The range registers lowest in January (15° C) and highest in May (36° C). It is also a region fanned by monsoon. The northeast monsoon brings heavy and continuous rain from September to January, and the southwest monsoon, which is particularly persistent in the western part of the province, between May and August. In the eastern plains of Isabela, the average yearly rainfall amounts to 2,100 mm (PDA 1978:6–9). While the amount and intensity of rainfall brought by the northeast and southwest monsoons varies, all months of the year experience a number of rainy days. Thus, this part of northeastern Luzon in general experiences a less marked seasonality (Coronas 1920; Hernandez 1954; Flores and Balagot 1969). It is also estimated that 43 percent of the tropical cyclones that pass through the Philippines directly affect northern Luzon (Flores et al. 1969:173; Griffin 1984:99).

A plurality of agricultural families in Isabela continue to depend on cultivated lands, which are rented on a regular basis; approximately half of Isabela farmlands are either under part or full tenancy. Such a high tenancy ratio is due to the fact that large tracts of fertile land in the plains of western Isabela are still parcel lands owned by private corporations, mainly to grow tobacco. Isabela, however, is still a grain surplus province. In 1976, the effective crop area devoted to rice (T: *palay*) production was 171,285 ha and the overall yield was 2,400 kg (48 *cavan*) per hectare. The following year, corn ranked second to rice in production and value, with 74,205 ha of effective crop area and 950 kg of production per hectare. Tobacco, the most important cash crop, came third that year with an average yield of 1,074 kg (21.5 quintals) per hectare planted in 12,610 ha (PDA 1978:55–60).

The province of Isabela remained a frontier until the middle of this century; the Spanish colonial power failed to penetrate the area and to subdue the indigenous population who resisted Christianization (Keesing 1962:177). It was only during the eighteenth century that small waves of immigrants, mostly the Ilokano from the west coast of Luzon, entered the area in search of new land. Later, during the Philippine monopoly of tobacco trade with Spain (1781–1863), the rich and mineralized soil of Isabela attracted more pioneers to grow tobacco (McLennan 1980:112–18). However, parts of Isabela remained outside effective government control until the early decades of this century.

Events in the early decades of this century intensified immigration into Isabela. For example, the Americans completed the North Luzon Highway during the 1920s, which opened the sparsely populated headwaters of the Cagayan River to the crowded central Luzon plains. Continued land and population pressures in the plains of Luzon resulted in peasant revolts such as the Huk Rebellion before and after World War II. A large population, dissident or otherwise, came to Isabela to take refuge. Immigration continues today at an accelerated pace. One source indicates that from 1967 to 1977 Isabela experienced a net immigration of 24,590 people (PDA 1978:16–18).

In eastern Isabela the terrain rises to the saddle of the Sierra Madre range and falls to the beaches of the Philippine Sea. While the foothills of this range are geologically marine and terrestrial sediments, the Sierra Madre is mainly of volcanic origin and consists of basaltic and diorite rocks and occasionally of limestone formation (Barrera 1969:58; Antonio 1974:2). The elevation of this range in the province of Isabela varies from as low as 100 m up to 1,500 m, creating high angles of inclination in particular areas.

Until early in this century, the Sierra Madre in the province of Isabela was covered with tropical rain forest. This forest has been the source of timber

The Setting

and game since Spanish times (Blair and Robertson 1903–09, Vol. 18:98–99). Animal-powered logging, called carabao logging, exploited the hardwood for house, boat, or furniture construction. Small-scale commercial logging, particularly by the Japanese, began in the early decades of this century. Due to the problem of transportation, however, the commercial operation was concentrated only in a few coastal areas of northeastern Luzon (Goddard 1930:311). Thus, even in the later decades of this century, rain forest such as the Sierra Madre was described as being impenetrable (see Jurika 1962:51).

Today, the forest area of the Sierra Madre is shrinking. As the international and domestic lumber demand increased in the 1950s, widespread commerical logging began in the area. The opening of highways coupled with access to leftover heavy machinery after World War II further intensified the logging. Today, Isabela ranks as one of the top log-producing provinces in the country, and the first in Luzon. In 1977, approximately 6,000 km^2 (57% of the total land area of the province) was officially designated as forest land. In 1978, fourteen logging concessions operating in the province covered a total forest area of approximately 5,000 km^2 (83% of the total forest area). The official estimation of the total lumber production for that year in the province of Isabela came to 100 million board feet (PDA 1978:6, 65). In addition, geologists found that the Sierra Madre contained valuable minerals such as magnesium, copper, nickel and chromite. Following the logging companies, mining companies have entered the area (see Headland 1986:252). Because forest must be cleared before mining of such minerals begins, it has further intensified logging.

The valley (western) and coastal (eastern) watersheds of the Sierra Madre differ in topography. In general, the valley watershed is comparatively broader and gentler in terrain; the rivers are part of the Cagayan River tributary system, thus giving the terrain a somewhat complicated formation. On the coastal side, the rivers empty directly into the Philippine Sea; thus, the hills run at right angles to the ridge of the Sierra Madre. These topographic differences of the two watersheds, compounded by slight climatic variations, have resulted in a two different forest communities (see Allen 1985:49). The valley watershed is also more heavily logged. This is partly due to easy access from the highways. Loggers also claim that the forest on the valley watershed produces more export-quality logs per unit of forest area than the coastal forest.

The logging trails that crisscross the valley watershed are used for shuttle transportation between remote places and the highways. On the other hand, the coastal areas of Isabela, which until the 1920s were considered to be more accessible (by boat) than the valley side, have become, in terms of relative accessibility, more remote. Single engine planes that offer services to particular coastal towns are both erratic and expensive. Motorboats, which frequent these coastal towns to deliver consumer goods and to haul local produce, are unsafe to ride during most of the year. Hiking across the Sierra Madre is most of the time the only reliable alternative, requiring at the least an arduous two-day journey.

Due to hostile terrain and remoteness, the agricultural population along the 200-kilometer shoreline of the province of Isabela is relatively sparse. Except in the Palanan Bay area, where ecclesiastical groups such as the Franciscans have had missions since the seventeenth century (Keesing 1962:258; see also Headland 1986:201–13), the river terraces and plateaus of the coastal watershed in Isabela have been settled only since the 1950s.

San Mariano, one of the 37 municipalities of the province of Isabela, is perhaps the largest in the country. It is located on the valley watershed of the Sierra Madre and has a total land area of approximately 1,500 km^2. Physiographically, it is divided by the inhabitants into two areas. The northern half, called the "small stream area," is composed of three river valleys with an approximate drainage area of 700 km^2. To the south of this is the "big stream area," the boundary of which goes beyond the municipality of San Mariano and forms a 2,500 km^2 drainage area. The river terraces and rolling hills in between the river valleys form the human settlement area of the municipality.

San Mariano is still a frontier in the literal sense. Established as a municipality in 1923, it had a sparse population concentrated in a few barrios in the earlier half of this century. In 1977, there were approximately 2,700 people in the municipality, excluding the Agta and other seasonal residents. Typical of the province, approximately 50 percent of the permanent settlers were Ilokano, followed by Ibanag who make up 36 percent (MDS 1979:5–10). Ilokano along with the Ibanag control the economy and politics of this primarily Roman Catholic population. Ilokano is the trade language.

The intensity of logging operations in the province is perhaps nowhere greater than in the municipality of San Mariano. While 94 percent of the land area in the municipality was classifed as jungle in 1979, 63 percent of this jungle area was also concessioned out to six commercial logging companies. Ten saw mills operating with band mill machines in the municipality reported extraction of a total of 98,000 m^3 of logs in 1979 (Bureau of Forestry, San Mariano Station). It was estimated that the municipality drew an annual revenue of over a million pesos (in 1979, 7.50 pesos was equivalent to one U.S. dollar) from the logging industry.

The municipal town (T: *sentro*) of San Mariano is connected by a 21-kilometer all-season road from the North Luzon Highway. Besides being a market center, it houses the only church in the municipality. During the logging season, people from even remote barrios hitchhike on trucks to attend Sunday morning mass. Sunday is also a market day when consumer goods and local products are bought and sold. In the afternoon, as the market withers, men throng the cock-fighting arena, billiard hall or movie theatre. During the northeast monsoon floods, when logging activities stop, it is a one-day hike along the rivers from the remote barrios to get to town. Some resort to dug-out canoes or bamboo rafts to travel. To transport goods, wooden sleds or carts pulled by water buffalo are used. When typhoons hit the area or when rivers are heavily flooded, travel can become impossible.

The Study Population

Since the entire length of the Sierra Madre range is inhabited by various Negrito groups, eastern Luzon carries a sizable proportion of the Negritos in the Philippines (see Fox and Flory 1974). Schebesta (1952–57) estimated that 8,000 Negritos were concentrated in eastern Luzon. A total of 1,315 Negritos were listed in the Cagayan Valley alone in the 1939 census (Keesing 1962:220, 264). To my knowledge, no recent census,[1] including the one from 1970, has actually enumerated the Negrito population of northeastern Luzon.

My census enumeration shows that there are a total of 1,644 Agta Negritos concentrated in eight municipalities along the Sierra Madre in Isabela (see Appendix 1). Populations were more concentrated in three municipalities (Palanan, Maconacon and Divilacan) of the coastal watershed and one municipality (San Mariano) of the valley watershed (see Map 1). Approximately two-thirds of the population (1,203) lived in a relatively narrow belt of the coastal watershed. At the time of the census taking, the Agta of Isabela inhabited 42 of the numerous river valleys; river valleys are defined here as those valleys formed by rivers that directly discharge either into the ocean or the major rivers. Eight river valleys carried most of the Agta population, the highest concentration being located in the Palanan River valley. The study of their settlement pattern showed that the Agta of Isabela were scattered among eighty camps.

There are observable disparities in the settlement patterns among the Agta groups of the valley and coastal watersheds of the Sierra Madre. In general, the Agta of Isabela live an average of five kilometers from the next nearest Agta camp, seven kilometers from the nearest agricultural settlement and eight kilometers from the nearest logging camp; wherever possible, they live along or near logging roads. However, the coastal watershed Agta live closest to agricultural settlements (3.8 km) and the valley watershed Agta live farthest from such settlements (13 km). It will be shown later that these differences in the settlement patterns affect the degree of social and economic interaction between the Agta and non-Agta populations.

The Agta of the valley and coastal watersheds also show differential aptitudes for horticultural activities. During my 1979–1980 stay, 92 percent of the Agta families interviewed claimed to have practiced some form of swiddening in that agricultural year. However, while 96 percent of the Agta families living on the coastal side had practiced subsidiary swidden activity, only 80 percent of the families of the valley watershed claimed to have done so.

The Agta group inhabiting the Disabungan River drainage of San Mariano on the valley watershed of the Sierra Madre was chosen to be the subject for detailed study. The decision to select this group, called here the Disabungan Agta, is partly rooted in the pattern of anthropological research among the Agta Negritos. Most of the anthropological research on the northeastern Luzon Agta, which were cited above, have concentrated on the coastal groups. Only a few researchers (e.g., Barbosa 1988; Clark 1986) have studied the groups living on the valley watershed, and with the exception of these and brief accounts by Semper (1861, 1869), Schebesta (1952–57) and Keesing (1962), nothing has been written on them.

Moreover, because the forests of the valley watershed in general and San Mariano in particular are heavily logged today, they provide a more dramatic situation for the study of environmental change of the Agta forest homeland. The valley watershed Agta in general tend to depend more heavily on forest resources than their coastal counterparts, who have access to the open sea for marine resources. Thus, the forest encroachment has had more direct consequences for the subsistence pattern of the valley watershed Agta.

The Disabungan Agta are concentrated in three river valleys, and at any given time they live in an average of six camps. In late 1979, they numbered 138 (67 males and 71 females). The Disabungan Agta (henceforth Agta unless otherwise specified) are perhaps the most consistent hunters of the Isabela groups. This group also claims to have the lowest percentage (59%) of households practicing shifting cultivation in a given year.

PART II

THE TRADITIONAL WORLD

4
The Natural Environment

Any description of change of a human society is valid only in reference to particular points in time. To understand the change among the Agta, the Agta system is divided here into traditional and transitional worlds. This part of the study addresses the traditional world by describing those various components of the Agta system which existed prior to the introduction of non-foraging economic strategies, and which are in substantial part still intact today. In general, the description of the traditional world emphasizes the morphostatic aspects of the Agta system. In the next section, which focuses on the transitional world, the components of the Agta system that were introduced in recent times will be discussed, and the morphogenetic aspect of the transitional world will be emphasized.

Environment

Cultural and human ecologists frequently use the term "environment" to mean only the natural environment. Suggesting that culture is a tool that people use to interact with their environment, they define environment as the physical and material surroundings that enter into relationships with human beings. Human ecologists in particular further argue that the material relations of a human population can be described with little reference to the views of the world entertained by its members (Vayda and Rappaport 1968). Other anthropologists, who have traditionally believed that culture is a coherent system in its own right and not a mere tool to exploit the physical environment, find this meaning of environment narrow.

The more popular definition of environment in anthropology glosses over the distinction between nature and culture on the thesis that their relationship is very intricate (see Hutterer 1985:55–58). Moreover, this view claims on the methodological level that the boundaries between natural and cultural components cannot be clearly delineated. According to this view, environment encompasses not only space and habitat but also the sociocultural milieu and the human groups beyond but within the experiential field (Helm 1962:633). It is this definition that is used here to mean environment.

Although the natural and sociocultural realms are difficult to distinguish, their existence as separate theoretical entities cannot be argued against. These two entities interact at different levels within human systems such as the Agta. The analysis of these interactional relationships is important if one is to understand the environment of a society. And to understand the interrelationships of the environmental components, a systemic description of the environment is required (Anderson 1973; Ellen 1979; Hutterer 1985).

A systemic description of the environment of a society like the Agta can be done from either the investigator's or the insider's point of view. Because the investigator and the insider order the importance of the environmental components differently, they differ in their understanding and evaluations of these components (Conklin 1961:27). Thus, depending upon the perspective, the environment of a society can be described differently. In describing the natural environment, an investigator analyzes what could be called the scientific environment of the group being studied according to the tenets of Western natural history (Silberbauer 1981:259–60), describing the hills, forests, rivers, plants, animals, etc., of the group's ecosystem irrespective of their meaning to the people.

The insider, on the other hand, views the environment very differently. Within the potentially exploitable *operational environment* (Rappaport 1969a:186) of the group, there are only certain tracts which are regularly exploited. This regularly exploited area, which I call here the *utilized environment*, provides most of the material resources for the group. On the other hand, many of the natural resources of the utilized environment have little direct relevance to the group. For example, the mineral ore underneath the ground (for which groups like the Agta lack the technology to extract), or an edible plant (which is not eaten for cultural reasons) means very little to the group. Further, the physical boundary of their ecosystem may not coincide with the existential boundary of their sociocultural system. Within a group's sociocultural world, some features that are pertinent to an outside observer are not recognized, or at least have very restricted meaning. In short, the insider's view of the environment includes most importantly the culturally meaningful part of the physical (i.e., utilized) and sociocultural environment.

The Utilized Environment

The Agta occupy a relatively large rain forest homeland. The total area of the operational environment of the Disabungan Agta is approximately 600 km^2 (see Allen 1985:46). The elevation of this forest area ranges from 100 rivers, each having an average annual water runoff of approximately 300 million m³ (NWRC 1976:15).

The utilized environment of the Disabungan Agta makes up about forty percent of the operational environment. Hence, the actual utilized environment area is approximately two square kilometers per person. In physiography, the utilized area tends to be lower in elevation (ranging up to 800 m, and most frequently below 500 m), and has in general a lower degree of incline. Only two of the three river valleys are inhabited on a regular basis and the forest area adjacent to these river banks are those most often exploited. In short, the Agta utilized environment excludes areas which are either of higher elevations and inclines or located away from the river course.

Most of the utilized area of the Disabungan Agta lies within what is called the lowland tropical rain forest. The biotic communities of such rain forests are known to have a very high diversity of species (Richards 1979:3–4; Marten 1984). For example, in the Philippine rain forests, there are approximately 1,600 identified genera and over 8,000 identified species of plants (Merrill 1967:61). In northeastern Luzon in particular, the forest is dominated by at least eleven species of dipterocarps. Second-story undergrowth and the forest floor are represented by various species of trees, shrubs and vines (Allen 1985:50).

For the hunting and gathering Agta groups, the forest (*télon*) is the most important life line. The diversity and complexity of the forest thus have strong influences on the Agta traditional world. Due to the high diversity of the rain forest communities, most plant resources are dispersed throughout the forest. While all areas tend to provide a nexus of plant resources for human consumption, it is not a rich ecosystem for specific plant foods (Hutterer 1983:179; Rambo 1982:261; Headland 1987). In addition, the complexity of the rain forest communities brings further variability by dictating a somewhat uneven availability of some of these plant resources. For example, lowland dipterocarp and high altitude montane forests differ in their structural compositions (Merrill 1945:83). Even the hill slopes and river terraces have different floristic compositions; the stream vegetation tends to have fewer tall trees (Whitford 1906:414) and more shrubs and herbs (Allen 1985:50).

The Agta have knowledge of, and names for, several hundred of the approximately 3,000 plant species in their environment (cf. Headland 1981:14–17). Of these numerous plant species recognized by the Agta, fewer than 300 plants have direct economic use or symbolic value to the group. Further, Agta claim that they depend on the regular exploitation of fewer than 100 plant species and approximately 50 food species.

A folk taxonomic study of the Agta shows that they divide the plant kingdom into three life form categories, namely "grass and herbacious plants" (*lamon*), "climbing and trailing plants or vines" (*lanot*), and "woody plants and trees" (*kayo*) (Headland 1981:24). Agta adults generally readily recognize and distinguish the generic and specific levels of those plants which have more direct economic, cultural or symbolic value to humans and food value to game animals (see Allen 1985:60). Agta wild plant resources come from all the above three life-form levels. For example, Agta exploit a number of grasses such as fern (*pako, Diplazium esculentum*)[1], wild chili (*sili, Capsicum minimum*), and elephant grass (*bigiw, Miscanthus* sp.). They extensively exploit a number of vines such as rattan (*uway, Calamus* spp.), a variety of palm (e.g., *nénga, Calamus* sp.), varieties of wild tuber (e.g., *ilus, Discorea* sp.), and betel leaf (*géwid, Piper betlé*). They also use a number of trees: tree fruits (e.g., *pélluat, Nephelium lappaceum*), areca nut (*butag, Areca* spp.), one palm variety (*anaw, Livistina* sp.), wild banana (*bigit, Musa* sp.) and bamboo (*bulo, Schizostachym* spp.).

The tropical rain forest like that of the Agta is largely a plant biomass (Pianka 1978:296); per unit, it contains less animal biomass than plant biomass. Of the animals, the largest portion are invertebrates and among vertebrates, arboreal animals predominate (Hutterer 1985:62–63). Further, due to the insular nature of the Philippine Islands' forests, there are even fewer mammals and reptiles (see Alcala 1976:139; Mudar 1985:69) that could form the animal resources of the Agta. The inventory of Disabungan Agta terrestrial game animals comprises only six species of mammals (wild pig, deer, monkey, palm civet, civet cat and fruit bat), two reptiles (python and monitor lizard) and various species of birds.

While we know little about the Agta ethnozoology, observation shows that Agta distinguish four types of animals, namely, "walking animals" (*hayup*), "crawling animals" (*ulag*), "flying animals" (*manok*) and "aquatic animals" (*ikkan*). The walking animals include most of the prey species of the Agta such as wild pig (*léman, Sus barbatus philippinensis*; see Mudar 1985), deer (*ugsa, Cervus philippinensis*), monkey (*buhog, Macaca philippinensis*), palm civet (*ales, Paradoxurus philippinensis*), and civet cat (*musang, Vivera tangalunga*). The crawling animals include python (*biklat, Python reticulatus*), monitor lizard (*bénnég, Varanus salvator*) and various species of snakes and insects. The flying animals include all bird species, including the wild chicken (*italon, Gallus gallus*). Aquatic animals are represented by several varieties of fish (e.g., *kulapia, Tilapia* sp.; *délag, Ophicephalus* sp.), shrimp (*udang, Macrobrachium* sp.), eel (*igit, Anguilla* sp.), crocodile (*bukahot, Crodilus* sp.).

The Agta body of knowledge for animals they prey upon is more extensive than for non-prey (Mudar 1985). Agta use specific terms for prey species such as pig, deer and monkey as opposed to generic terms used for several species of economically less important animals. They semantically recognize not only the species but also the sex and age of large game animals. For example, the generic taxon "wild pig" is subdivided into three categories: the male adult (*butakal*), the female adult (*ténid*) and the young or young adult (*béhék*). The taxa "deer," "monkey," and "wild chicken" are similarly subdivided (see Headland et al. 1974:29, 106).

Because the Agta depend heavily on plant and animal resources, the biotic component of the environment constitutes a major chunk of their knowledge (Berlin 1978:9). The Agta nonetheless possess a rather intimate knowledge of the abiotic component of their environment. It seems that a large part of their knowledge of the abiotic component is derived from their use of space and perception of meteorological fluctuation.

The climate of the northeastern Luzon rain forest, including Isabela, where the Agta homeland is located, is virtually nonseasonal (see Hutterer 1983) in the sense that it registers a consistently high humidity (the mean annual humidity is 87%), high rainfall (a minimum of 100 mm per month), and high temperature (in an average 25° C).[2] The range of climatic variation is so small that it is buffered from any major vegetative and animal resource fluctuations; to a large extent, it maintains the same balance of species as well as the overall structure and composition of species year round (Richards 1979:138).

While the Agta experience little fluctutation in their natural resources, they perceive a seasonality in their climate. They tend to polarize the microvariations in the local climate and recognize seasons in their environment (see also Estioko-Griffin 1984:192–93; Allen 1985:53).

The wet season (*amian*), as characterized by the Agta, is a relatively short period of the year, when the area experiences continuous but slow rain. Such rains are occasionally preceded by lightning and thunder and can easily develop into a tropical depression. Particularly in the earlier months of this period there are strong winds or typhoons (*bagyo*) from the east. More frequently floods (*bihéng*) make rivers uncrossable. Even when it is not raining, clouds or fog may cover the sky. If the sky is clear, nights can bring heavy dews. The daily temperature fluctuates considerably; the day can be warm and the night very cold.

The dry season (*késinag*), according to Agta informants, constitutes the longer period of the year, when it is hot in mid-day. There are also frequent drizzles and often times heavy but intermittent rain. Short periods of flooding are not uncommon. Toward the end of the dry season, cyclones and typhoons are expected, which can in turn bring considerable rain.

The wet season coincides with the northeast monsoon season (October–January) and the dry season with the southwest monsoon season (May–August). Thus, while meteorologically speaking, only the intensity of the rainfall varies across seasons, the Agta themselves contrast the continuous rain of the wet season from the intermittent but heavy rain of the dry season and see a seasonality in their environment.

The Agta occasionally find it hard to guess when the season changes. They thus supplement their assessment of such changes by the flowering or fruiting of particular plants or by birds' (e.g., *bélisgogo*) song. However vaguely defined, these seasons are also important calendar markers in the Agta life. Residential histories and other events like birth, death, raid or typhoon are recounted in reference to these seasons. Their perception of climatic fluctuation brings some changes in the settlement pattern of the Agta; the groups tend to localize and nucleate their camps during the wet season. Because of the difficulty in trading due to the more frequent floods in this season, the Agta temporarily depend more on the forest resources than on outside trade.

The Agta are called upon to make a variety of adjustments within one season. Because daily climatic fluctuations affect the Agta foraging strategy, they have perfected techniques of predicting weather through color, formation and movements of the clouds, as well as the direction of the wind. The possibility of flood is judged from the intensity of rain in the upriver areas and the muddiness of the river. On the basis of these forecasts, Agta make day-to-day decisions.

5
The Social Groupings

The Agta do not use all of the potentially exploitable animal and plant resources of their physical environment, and they rank those resources they do use according to their relative importance. Similarly, the Agta do not recognize all the human members of their sociocultural world equally; they categorize them into various groupings and interact with them in differential degrees. Two important criteria for these categories are kinship and residence.

The adaptation of the Agta to their nonseasonal rain forest environment plays an important part in their sociocultural environment. In the following pages, I will describe the sociocultural aspects of the Agta traditional world. The order in which these components are described does not necessarily assume a strong causal relationship.

Kinship

To anthropologists, kinship is an inclusive term for the conceptual spheres of marriage and descent (Keesing 1975:22). Kinship to the Agta is the most important criterion of the cognitive structure. As a major organizing principle of their world, kinship permeates almost all aspects of their life. Agta say: "a person without kin is a dead person." Kinship provides principles that relate or oppose individuals, and by putting individuals into more or less exclusive categories, it assigns roles to them. Cumulatively, kinship defines the specific behavior of an Agta individual in relation to others.

The kinship system among the Agta is bilateral; that is to say they trace serial affiliation from both parents and recognize all people related by genealogical ties without particular emphasis on either patrilineal or matrilineal connections (Murdock 1960:2). As will be made clear in the following pages, the Agta kin categorization is egocentric (and not ancestorcentric). Therefore, the range of kin recognition varies from one individual (or a sibling set) to another. At the same time, the Agta individuals in a group are closely interrelated. That the Agta society is not divided into discrete units such as clans and lineages is not seen as a problem by the Agta themselves. Indeed, due to this, there is social cohesion, continuity and order (Appell 1976:7). For the Agta, kin categories are well defined; they readily recognize and divide members of their society into a number of categories (see Fig. 1).

In kinship, focus for an Agta is him- or herself. An ego recognizes both consanguineal and affinal ties. The consanguineal relatives, who are related to ego by birth, are traced through both the father and mother and sons and daughters. They include both lineal and collateral consanguines. Affinal relatives are those directly related by the marriage of ego or of ego's lineal consanguines; it excludes, for example, ego's spouse's cousin. Any individual who falls within this kin recognition is categorized as kin and anyone, even members of one's own camp group, who falls beyond this range is categorized as non-kin. The distinction between kin and non-kin determines much of Agta interpersonal interaction.

The members within the kin category form the kin group, who are primarily recruited by birth relations. Secondarily, non-kin become kin through marriage relation. An Agta's kin group is not, however, an ever-expanding number of people. In reality, the number of kin recognized by an ego remains fairly small. As elder kin die, an Agta tends to forget collateral consanguines linked by ties beyond three ascending generations. Offspring of such consanguines thus become non-kin. The death of a lineal consanguine (e.g., father's brother) severs kinship ties to affines (e.g., father's brother's widow). In short, ego acquires a new set of relationships to a new group of people by marriage, and loses old sets of relationships through death (Schusky 1972:89). In this way, the kin category of the Agta remains small.

In addressing kin, Agta generally use polysemic terms to designate not just one but several structurally related categories of kin. For example, for all those in ego's generation, sibling terms of address are used and all children of these people are addressed as *children* (*anak*). Generational terminology is also used for relatives of second ascending and second descending generations; both grandparents and grandchildren are addressed by one single term (*apo*). In contrast, the terms of reference to ego's own, parental, and child generations are lineal (see Appendix 4). In the parental generation, parents are differentiated from parents' siblings and males from females. In ego's generation, elder siblings are distinguished from younger (but no gender discrimination is made) and siblings are distinguished from cousins.[1] The relatives of the child generation are distinguished only as lineals and collaterals. Only a very few non-kin (those who tend to live in ego's camp, e.g., wife's sister's husband, husband's brother's wife), are addressed by kin terms.

The division between kin and non-kin is crucial in that it is on this distinction that the Agta marriage rules are promulgated. The Agta do not have any

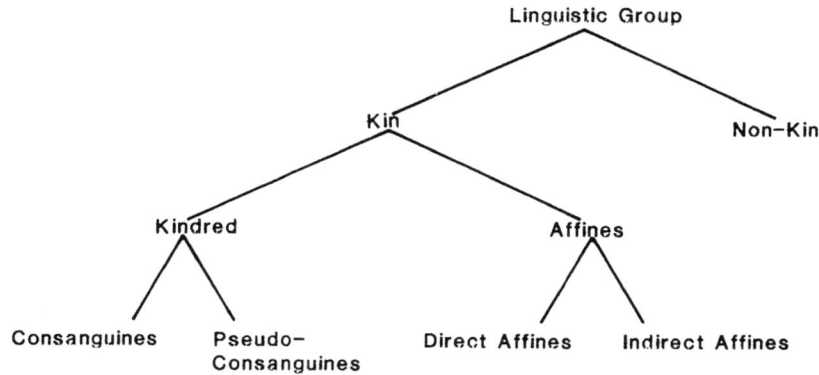

FIGURE 1. Diagram of Agta kin categories.

specific prescriptive or preferential marriage norms, whether in terms of kinship or residence. As we shall see later, they have a wider definition of incest, which prohibits sexual relations between an ego and any kin—consanguineal or affinal. Generally, they should not marry persons linked by a kinship term of reference. Thus, they are expected to find their marriage mates among Agta who are non-kin. The distinction between kin and non-kin is also maintained in that non-kin are distrusted and avoided in social relations.

Within the kin category of the Agta, the distinction between consanguinity and affinity is somewhat complicated. Normally, all individuals who are married to ego or his/her consanguines are, by conventional anthropological definition, affines. Agta, however, extend consanguineal kin terms to all affines except ego's spouse and spouse's consanguines and ego's child's spouse. Because the Agta extend consanguineal kinship terms to such affines, these affines become "pseudo-consanguines." Thus "affine" becomes a restricted category. The expanded consanguineal category (including both consanguines and pseudo-consanguines) is here termed *kindred* (e.g., Mitchell 1963:351; King 1976:126; Appell 1976:124). The restricted category of affinal kin is here called *affines*.

The distinction between kindred and affines is another important principle of Agta kinship structure which dictates their interpersonal relations. Ego's kindred, as defined here, is neither a residential nor obligatory unit in itself. The differentiation of kindred members, on the basis of the degree of genealogical relationship, specify the obligatory relationships. The affines who may not have any concurrent genealogical relationship among themselves are, on the other hand, grouped together by ego because they all have marital links to ego or to ego's immediate consanguines (viz., siblings, children, siblings' children). Among the Disabungan Agta, four types of affines are recognized in the kin terminology: father- or mother-in-law, son- or daughter-in-law, brother- or sister-in-law and child's spouse's parent.

Members of both kindred and affinal categories are kin to ego and thus, according to the Agta incest rule, they are not eligible for marriage. There is, however, one exception to this rule; ego may marry certain affines (e.g., spouse's sibling). Agta serial monogamy often involves sisters and the majority of cases of polygyny are sororal (see Estioko-Griffin 1984:27–28). There are also a few cases of sister exchange and of a pair of brothers marrying sisters. In one case, a woman reportedly married her daughter's widower. The incest rule for kindred category remains more difficult to violate. In actuality, a few cases of cousin marriages have been documented.

Agta make further distinctions among affines, and observe different behavioral proscriptions. They differentiate the affines into what could be called direct affines and secondary, or indirect affines. Direct affines are ego's spouse's siblings, spouse's parents and ego's sibling's spouses, while secondary affines are affines of ego's lineal consanguines (other than siblings). An ego must avoid using the birth name (*ngahan*) of his direct affine and instead use either a kin term or an alternate name (*sangay*) usually coined by ego. Further, if ego is a male, he must maintain a formal respect relationship with his direct affines irrespective of their age; the female ego shows only a minimal respect to her direct affines. The direct affines do not reciprocate in name avoidance or respect relationships with an ego. This asymmetrical relationship is maintained perhaps to discourage sororate marriages, which nonetheless occur. Secondary or indirect affines, on the other hand, are those to whom and by whom no naming proscription and respect relationship is called for. Among kin, the indirect affines are least trusted and are often avoided in social interaction.

Agta kinship thus recognizes individuals of five categories: consanguines, pseudo-consanguines, direct affines, secondary or indirect affines, and non-kin. To the Agta, these categories are mutually exclusive at a given time. By being a member of one particular category, the Agta individual in relation to another individual is expected to have a particular interpersonal relationship. By defining the structural groups and their given behavioral correlates, Agta kinship provides the axis as well as the criterion for their social groupings. And since kinship crosscuts the boundaries of residence, it has important consequences for the Agta settlement pattern.

Settlement Pattern

Ties of contiguity, like kinship, are central to members of most societies. The precise relationship between kinship and settlement pattern, however, varies from society to society. Among the Agta, the kinship relationship is the determining factor in their settlement pattern and is reflected in their five levels of socioresidential units. In the order of their inclusiveness, they are: the linguistic group, the watershed group, the river valley group, the band, and the household; each of them will be defined in the following pages.

It has been shown above that, from the point of view of an Agta individual, members of society fall into discrete categories such as kin and non-kin. However, when multiple Agta members are concerned, their overlapping aggregates necessarily expand to include a large number of people; there is the interlocking kinship network that binds these people together and distinguishes them with groups who maintain separate kinship network. All the Agta members who belong within the maximal extent of one such interlocking kinship network make up the highest level of the Agta socioresidential unit. As will be shown later, this unit is not a territorial group that defends its territory or controls its resources. The members occupy a particular forest area primarily to maintain economic, social and political isolation from their counterparts. Since there is no permanent kinship link between one such group and the other neighboring groups, there is also little interaction and communication among them. Consequently, one such group differs from others in language (see Appendix 3) as well as in a few other sociocultural practices. I will call this level of socioresidential unit of the Agta a *linguistic group*. There are four such linguistic groups in Isabela (see Appendix 2). The nature of interrelation between the linguistic groups will be discussed in detail in Chapter 7.

The homeland area of a particular linguistic group usually stretches across both the watersheds of the Sierra Madre range. While extensive kinship, marriage, and other social ties are maintained among members of a linguistic group living across the watersheds, the regular economic exchanges are maintained only minimally because of the greater physical distance involved. Thus, the members of a linguistic group are usually divided into two economically independent *watershed groups* (these must not be confused with Agta populations from other linguistic groups inhabiting the same Sierra Madre watershed). The watershed group, as a subunit of the linguistic group, is simply a more closely interacting group of people; the interaction within the members of a watershed group is more intensive and the communication more efficient. These watershed groups also differ in their subsistence patterns as they have differing access to marine resources. They patronize separate—coastal or valley—agricultural settlements for purposes of barter trade. Among the four Agta linguistic groups in Isabela, there are seven such watershed groups; one linguistic group is represented by only one watershed group. The Disabungan Agta, the group under detailed study, is a watershed group.

Within one watershed group, Agta further identify themselves with particular river valleys (valleys formed by rivers that directly discharge into the ocean or the major rivers). The members of a *river valley group* tend to locate their residences within one particular river valley for most of the year and over a long period of time. This population is an even more closely interacting group; the members pay regular visits to one another, and economic exchanges are more frequent. They may occasionally come together to collectively hunt or fish. They often cross one another's path in camp movements, alternate the use of the same campsites, and may nucleate in one campsite to spend the months during the northeast monsoon floods. A river valley group, in fact, occupies and exploits one single Agta utilized environment area. Agta families may leave such a river valley to reside elsewhere, temporarily or permanently, but they usually continue to regard this valley as their home (see Estioko-Griffin 1984:31).

The river valley group of Agta is further divided into *bands*. This term is used here without its connotation of territorial ownership and fixed membership[2] to simply denote an aggregate of Agta members, who reside in one single camp at a given time (see Damas 1969a:197–211; see also Headland 1986:10), primarily because the members are related to one another by close kinship, often lineal and direct affinal ties.

In Isabela, one Agta river valley group contains one to eight such bands which, on the average, maintain a physical distance of five kilometers from the next nearest band. Of the different levels of socioresidential units, the Agta band is the most easily defined social and physical entity. Although its membership fluctuates, a band has a core number of households that tend to stay together. Noting the fluctuation, Peterson writes that familiarity with the locale rather than genealogical relationship is the criterion of Agta band membership (1978a:11). To the Agta, however, whose sociocultural world is largely defined by kinship, the interlocking kin relationship forms the basis for band membership. The band, by most criteria, is the minimal economically viable unit. Agta pool their labor and allocate their resources to members at this band level.

The bands occupy a number of suitable campsites for varying lengths of time. In the Disabungan River drainage, campsites are located at varying elevations ranging from 150 m to 400 m. The Agta use two kinds of campsites, those located at river banks and jungle. Their coastal counterparts also use beaches, particularly near river mouths.

During most months in a year, the Disabungan Agta occupy various campsites along the river and the majority of them at the confluence (*pagbigin*). When it is too hot, or if foraging activity requires it, they move to jungle camps. Sometimes a combination of both the river bank and nearby jungle terrace is used. Whenever Agta dependence on the outside agricultural population is called for, they live in camps not very far from an agricultural settlement. But again, intensive interaction may lead to interethnic hostility and Agta respond by moving away from such settlements. The Disabungan

Agta live on the average of thirteen kilometers away from the agricultural settlement areas and five kilometers away from the logging stations, both of which serve as Agta trade nuclei.

At the advent of the typhoon season in August, Agta forest camps must be abandoned for fear of falling trees during the rain storms. As soon as the northeast monsoon approaches, the river bank camps must be moved to higher ground with open spaces. As travel becomes difficult during flooding and outside dependence is unreliable, Agta prefer upriver camps, where relatively intensive forest dependence is possible. Because all Agta swidden fields are upriver from the agricultural settlements and there are not that many suitable sites for camps in the flooding season, a number of Agta bands of one river valley may nucleate in one particular area. Thus, in the northeast monsoon season, while the distance between an Agta camp and agricultural settlement increases, the Agta intercamp distance decreases. As social visits are more intensified, sharing of food and labor across camps becomes common. These bands, which are sometimes camped less than a kilometer apart, may merge and temporarily form a larger band, giving an impression that the band size is bigger. Such nucleation of Agta bands brings its own social cost. Because the larger population is concentrated in a small area, there is a higher possibility of interaction, and consequently dissent, between non-kin. As Agta find this situation socially stressful, the bands cannot remain nucleated for more than two months. As soon as the flooding season subsides, the Agta disperse and live in separate distant camps.

An Agta band tends to maintain an optimum number of families and individuals. In Isabela, an average band is composed of five families (over half of the bands were formed by three to five families), or about 21 people. In the Disabungan area, Agta live in bands of three to eight families.

The family is the lowest socioresidential unit of the Agta. While a family is economically dependent on other households of the band, it maintains its separate hearth. While it does not always control the labor of its family members or the resources produced by them, a household functions as a decision-making unit.

Agta families are predominantly nuclear. That is, a typical family consists of one married couple and their unmarried children. To put this in the dyadic frame of reference (see Buchler and Selby 1968:29), a typical Agta family is composed of conjugal, parental and sibling dyads. In Isabela, 58% ($N = 400$) of the families are of this type.

The second most common family organization is the non-nuclear type, where the members possess only a conjugal dyad (without parental and sibling dyads) or only a paternal or maternal dyad (without conjugal dyad). In most cases, a single individual or only two unmarried siblings constitute such a non-nuclear family. This variation represents 28% of the Isabela Agta families.

Agta extended families include a couple in the parental generation, their unmarried as well as married children and their spouses. That is, there are conjugal dyads in both the parent and the child generations. Six percent of the Agta families in Isabela fall into this category. The remaining 8% of the Agta families fall into an *augmented* category. Most typically, this consists of a non-nuclear family sharing the hearth with another nuclear or non-nuclear family.

An Agta household occupies one lean-to (*belay*). If the members include many adults or more than one married couple, they may possess one additional lean-to. Lean-to type, its size and the construction materials are specific to campsites and the time of year. In general, Agta live in small, rectangular lean-tos (*pinanahang*). The frame of the lean-to is made up of two crossed poles, over which six to ten parallel poles are arranged. While fronds of at least seven varieties of palms are used for roofing material, one species in particular (*nénga*, *Livistina* sp.), which is the most durable, pliable, and fire resistent, is commonly used. The lean-to is propped up by a supporting pole and the floor is cleared of pebbles.

The Agta lean-to has been called an architectural wonder (Bennagen 1969a:51). It can be turned, raised or lowered to avoid sun, rain or wind. While a typical lean-to provides less than two square meters of living area, the household members and their dogs as well as visiting guests are accommodated. Its poles provide a convenient place to hang food items or other family possessions. Cooking is done by hanging a pot from the main supporting pole. A lean-to location can be changed every few days and transported by one person to another short distance campsite. A new one can easily be built by one person in three to four hours. Each Agta family keeps one such lean-to in many different campsites along the river valley so that they do not have to build a new one after every camp move.

In the typhoon season, lean-tos are tied to rocks or stones. When the heavy rain due to the northeast monsoon becomes more frequent, variations of lean-tos are built. For example, in a type called *kubo*, two lean-tos are combined to provide more living space. Or, they may live in thatched houses with raised platforms (*sahung*), which require a minimum of 20 hours to make. In spite of their relative permanency, these houses become infested with cockroaches and fleas. As soon as the northeast monsoon flood ends, Agta cheerfully abandon these houses, moving to river banks to live in lean-tos.

Along a river bank or in a spacious jungle camp, the lean-tos are arranged in a single file facing the same direction. Moreover, Agta families place their lean-tos in a pattern that reflects the kinship network of the band; closely related families have closely placed lean-tos and a lean-to of a particular family is flanked by the lean-tos of the husband's and wife's relatives and

The Social Groupings

so on. That is, the lean-to distribution in a particular camp generally maps the genealogical relation of the Agta band.

Postmarital Residence

In what way do the lower levels of socioresidential units tie together to form a higher level unit? More precisely, how do households form a band, and bands, a river valley group, and so on? The answer lies in the Agta rules and preferences for postmarital residence.

Marriage among the Agta is more a complex process than an event. It is generally initiated by the boy. By the time he reaches puberty, he submits to aesthetic scarification of his body, dons colorful loincloths and lavishly decorates himself with ornaments of various kinds. He starts visiting relatives in camps where he happens to find girls to court (*mégibébe*). As he grows older, he may join a gang of boys to tour distant camps in search of a prospective marriage partner. Marriage proposal is made either in flowery language or sometimes in song. Betel nut (*émman*) is exchanged to indicate the willingness to marry. Agta informants state that fornication can take place at this stage.

In rare instances, the girl might elope (*méglépwang*) with the boy. In most cases however, a formal marriage proposal is made by the parents or guardians of the boy. A woman, preferably related to both parties, acts as a go-between. If no serious objection from the girl's parents is foreseen, the boy and his kin pay a visit to the girl's camp. In the betrothal palaver (*sakad*), which is one of the few formal occasions of the Agta, gifts of dried meat, rice, or liquor are made to the girl's kin amidst conversation full of allegorical euphemisms (Headland 1978:129–30). After this, the marital arrangement is considered irrevocable and the *in uxorem* right of the couple is recognized. Defaults such as sexual liaisons with other partners or elopement by the girl with another man are taken seriously and can be retaliated by murder.

The boy is required to go through a bride service (*serbi*) to complete his marriage obligations; it is said that only among the far northern Agta linguistic groups can the bride price be paid in lieu of bride service. Ideally the bride service should last "two seasons" (approximately one year) and the voluntary service may continue for another year. The bride service is an apprentice period designed to test the perserverance of the boy; he is expected to provide food for the girl's family by hunting and fishing and to help with the household chores. Sometimes the boy fails to meet these obligations and runs away, jeopardizing his marriage relationship.

Marriage negotiation is sometimes given formal social recognition by holding a wedding ceremony (*késal*) toward the end of the bride service period but never after the birth of the first child. Such solemnization, where the groom's close kin take the more active role, involves no ritual. Traditionally, it was celebrated by inviting kin of both the groom and bride and feasting them with a thick glutinous porridge made out of the starch of caryota palm (*agél, Caryota cumingii*) and meat.

A few of the Agta residence rules are jurally given. For example, during the mandatory bride service period, both partners are proscribed from having long-term residence elsewhere than with the wife's kin. (This holds not only for a man's first marriage, but for his second marriage to a previously unmarried woman). Of the Agta couples in Isabela who were in the bride service period, 84% ($N = 19$) followed the rule. Three couples, who were not residing with the wife's kin, were under continuing pressure to do so and to fulfill the bride service obligation. In the event that the couple is separated or one partner is widowed, he or she will reside with kindred. When a woman remarries, the couple will reside with the new husband's kin. The switch in the residence rule for women married for the second time and after, in which she resides with the husband's kin, is because there is no bride service obligation. This also occurs perhaps because a woman more than a man faces difficulty in remarriage and is willing to reside with the husband's kin.

The residence rules are, however, not jurally given to Agta couples who have completed their bride service obligations and who are still married to their first spouses. Thus, these couples, who comprise the majority, are called upon to make their own postmarital residence decisions.

The nonsedentary Agta families do not usually limit themselves to unilocal residences. Their bilateral social system also does not require adherence to a unilocal rule of residence (see Murdock 1960:14). The Agta practice a combination of uxorilocal (residence with wife's close kin), virilocal (residence with husband's close kin) and neolocal (residence in bands with either husband's or wife's distant kin) residence affiliations. Normatively, however, Agta prefer one postmarital residential arrangement over others. Peterson reported that 47% of the Agta couples in Palanan maintained uxorilocality following the birth of their first child, while 33% were virilocal and 19% neolocal (1978a:46). In a review of Peterson's report, Headland contradicted Peterson by saying that the Agta of both Palanan and Casiguran areas tend towards virilocality (1978:132).

The disagreement over the Agta postmarital residence pattern is partly rooted in a methodological problem. Theoretically, an Agta household has a number of options for residence affiliation at a given time. When marriage, remarriage, or death brings changes in the family's kinship network, the family is forced to reconsider the options. Such situations can frequently occur. In short, postmarital residence among the Agta is not a permanent but a situational arrangement. Interviewing such a household about its present postmarital residence can be misleading since its past residence affiliations are not taken into consideration. In fact, observation of actual residence behavior may not reflect the ideal residence rule either. When an Agta camp is composed of both kindred and affine households of a person, which is often the case, the classification of families into particular postmarital residence typologies can become difficult.

The Agta themselves do not see these problems. They consider only kin as potential co-residents, and prefer to use close kin in actual residence affiliation. That is, a particular couple considers the range of options and rank orders the options to make the decision on long-term residence affiliation. This, translated into actual Agta postmarital arrangements at a given time, can be statistically analyzed. But the arrangements are primarily due to the group's kinship network, which the Agta families analyze to make their long-term residence decisions.

In the case of an Agta woman, the complex process of long-term residence decisions can be illustrated in a flow chart (Fig. 2). The applicability of the flow chart[3] was tested out on 19 Disabungan Agta women, who were married to their first husbands and whose genealogies and marital as well as residential histories were known. The test was also conducted among 6 women from the Casiguran area (Headland, personal communication). The result shows that 12 of the 25 women chose to live with their married sisters over their other lineal kin, including brothers. Eleven married women, who had no married sisters but had brothers and/or parents, resided with the husband's kin. On this accidental sample, the chart correctly predicted the residence pattern of 92% (23/25) of the women.

Further, we took the mirror image of the chart and conducted a test on 29 men. It showed that 8 men resided in their wives' married sisters' camps. Of the 16 men, who had their own close kin as a choice, 13 did not live with them. The predictability of the flow chart for the residence decision among men was 90% (26/29).

Within a given category of kin (e.g., siblings, other lineal relatives), an Agta couple has a number options for co-residence. In such cases, other preference rules of residence are used. For example, if the choice is among kin of different generations, the kin of the closer degree of genealogical relation is preferred (viz., ego's generation over parent's generation over grandparent's generation). In the same generation, other attributes are considered. A woman prefers a female relative over a male, a full sibling over a half sibling, and an older sibling over a younger sibling. In rare cases, when a couple must look beyond their lineal or affinal kin, they live with collateral kin. These kinship bonds, however, are not strong and the couple may choose to move among distant relatives to form a neolocal residence.

The residence affiliation among the Agta thus shows an interesting pattern in that Agta households not only practice an ambilocal residence over a period of time, they also follow an alternating pattern of residence affiliation.

42   *Living in a Lean-to*

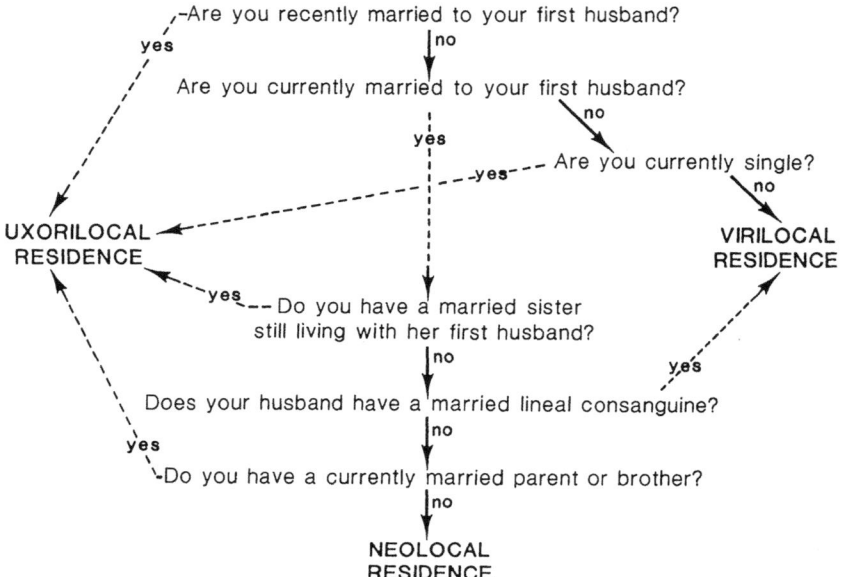

FIGURE 2. Chart showing residence choices of Disabungan Agta women.

For example, residence of a couple during bride service period is uxorilocal. If the wife has married sisters, the couple continues to be uxorilocal even after the bride service is completed. As these sisters remarry or die, the couple's residence becomes virilocal. If neither the husband nor the wife has close lineal relatives, they opt for neolocality and so on.

The composition of the Agta band is the direct result of the rules and preferences of postmarital residence decisions. When the composition of 42 of the 80 bands in Isabela were analyzed, it was found that 64% of the bands were formed primarily, although not exclusively, around sibling relationships. Parental relationships were predominant in the remaining bands. Of the band with a majority of sibling relationships, the sister-sister relationship was the most common (40%), followed closely by the brother-brother relationship (37%) (for the data on the Cagayan Agta, see Barbosa 1985:15; Estioko-Griffin 1984:29). In only 14% of the cases was the brother-sister bond predominant in camp residences. In bands with a majority of parental relationships, parent-daughter relationships made up 67% of the cases and parent-son relationships, 33%.

It can now be stated that the Agta kinship network connects socioresidential units at each level and to the higher levels. For example, a filiative link is required for a permanent membership of the Agta household. Close kin relationships are required to form a band. While kin relationships are closest among members of a band, they extend beyond the band level to form a river

The Social Groupings 43

valley group. A number of Agta river valley groups, which are interconnected by similar kin relationships form the watershed group and ultimately, the linguistic group.

In summary, the socioresidential groupings of the Agta are primarily an outcome of the kinship network of the group. Thus, one can argue that they are not formed in direct response to their physical environment *per se*. If these groupings are adaptive responses to the ecosystem, it is only in the sense that they are the most feasible structural arrangements for their given physical environment. When the people distribute themselves into the socioresidential groupings according to the rules of kinship and preferences in postmarital residence, the groups in turn distribute themselves in direct proportion to the resources. In addition, the Agta interact directly with their physical environment through other traditional sociocultural mechanisms, which are the topics of the following chapter.

6
The Forest Orientation

When and how the Agta adapted to the Philippine tropical rain forest remains speculative as the Agta Negrito prehistory is largely conjectural (see Griffin 1985a:86). The available archaeological evidence is scant, but indicates that human populations may have reached northeastern Luzon shortly after the end of the Pleistocene (12,000 B.P.) (Thiel 1980:89) and that by 6000 B.P, particular coastal areas were inhabited by semi-sedentary, horticultural populations (W. Peterson 1974). We do not yet know the nature of the relations of these populations with the Agta in terms of ethnogenesis or immigration history. Human genetic (see Omoto 1985) and linguistic studies (see Headland 1987b:13) do not help to clarify Agta ethnohistory. For example, we know little as to how the Agta were genetically or socioculturally related to the other Philippine Negrito groups. We have also yet to know the type of habitat from which they came and the kind of technological and economic organization they brought along.

Following the proposition by Hutterer (1982:134) that the tropical rain forest in general is a poor habitat for human plant foods, Headland (1987b) has argued that the Agta rain forest lacks sufficient quantity of wild yam, and therefore, the Agta did not live in the rain forest until they had established trade relationships with neighboring populations (i.e., according to Headland's estimate, around 2000 B.C.). This assertion, based on largely secondary and conjectural data, raises a number of questions. For example, we have yet to study the availability of plant foods, including yam, in the northeastern Luzon rain forest. While we know that the Agta had access to a number of starchy plant foods such as caryota palm, wild banana, and other starch-rich fruits (Allen 1985:56), we do not know what percentage of the Agta diet in the past was actually derived from plant resources in general, and wild yam in particular; we do not know the energy contribution of the Agta plant resources compared to the animal resources.

The available evidence indicates that the Agta have lived in the northeastern Luzon rain forest, even by the most conservative estimate, for at least 4,000 years. Ethnographic and ethnobotanical studies (Allen 1985) support the assertion that the Agta must have lived in the rain forest for a much longer time (see also Eder 1987:12). There is linguistic evidence to support this view (Headland 1981:15–17).

Today, when the Agta dependence on the outside world is increasing, most Agta bands continue to depend on forest resources. The presently available data does not negate the high probability that Agta in the past lived by hunting, gathering and fishing. Today, through a combination of these three foraging activities, they derive a substantial portion of their livelihood from the forest. The Disabungan Agta in particular derive 41% of the total caloric intake directly from the traditionally foraged foods (see Appendix 10). In short, the Agta were, and many of them still are, forest-oriented; and their forest orientation is most closely reflected in their exploitative technology and the rules of social organization.

Technology

Technology is used here not only in the tool sense but also in the labor sense (Binford 1980:13). That is, it includes both the tool-complex and the know-how as well as the behavior that surrounds it. The traditional technology of the Agta can be described under three modes, namely, hunting, gathering and fishing.

The technology of hunting is an important criterion that distinguishes the Agta from their non-Agta neighbors. Agta themselves claim, and their agricultural neighbours concur, that the Agta were and still are primarily hunters. I have described above that Agta semantically distinguish the generic and specific levels and gender as well as age sets of the game animals. They possess considerably detailed knowledge of the herd size, sex ratio, and age structure of game animals. As we will see later, hunting is relatively formalized and ritualized. In the Agta ranking of food items, the meat of wild animals falls in the most preferred category.

Hunting among the Agta is not, however, just a symbolically important activity. With the exception of a few coastal groups who rely on fishing for at least part of the year, hunting is consistently the most important Agta traditional subsistence activity. Hunting should have provided primary subsistence to most Agta groups in the past, and directly or indirectly, it still provides it today. The Disabungan Agta derive 23% of the caloric intake directly from the consumption of the meat of wild animals. In addition, approximately half of the meat of wild animals is traded to acquire domestic cereals, which form another important part of the Agta diet today. If the Agta did not trade the meat, the direct caloric contribution of hunting alone could account for half of their diet. When they are trading meat for cereals, the total caloric contribution of hunting and meat-related trade may come up to 80%. The fact that hunting is also a consistent activity across various months in a year is reflected in the Agta time allocation for this activity (see also Estioko-Griffin 1984: Table 6.11 for similar data). In general, the Disabungan Agta spend 48% of their working time[1] in hunting-related activities (see Appendix 6).

The hunting grounds of the Agta are generally the lowland and montane forests along hillsides and river banks (see also Allen 1985:54). The Disabungan Agta, who occasionally hunt in areas as high as 800 meters, generally frequent forest areas below 500 meters. The hunting radius of the Agta is not a circle that radiates equidistantly out of their campsite but a rectangle that covers mostly areas upriver from the camp. In most hunting trips, the circuit distance covered by an individual hunter is less than 25 kilometers.

Agta do not observe taboos on killing or eating any wild animals. Agta game animals include all locally available large terrestrial animals. Wild pig in particular, which is most abundant in their rain forest homeland, is favored as the most important large game. Deer comes second in the rank order of abundance as well as of the preferred game. During an observation period of 64 days, 60% ($N = 35$) of the large game killed by a band of Disabungan Agta were wild pigs as opposed to 26% deer (see Appendix 7; see also Griffin 1984:109; Estioko-Griffin 1984:185). In the random encounter by the author of the large game killed, 66% ($N = 44$) were again wild pigs. Python, which is the only non-human predator of large game in the forest, is occasionally killed and eaten. Other animals that are killed whenever encountered are monkey, monitor lizard and wild chicken. Agta also claim occasionally to hunt fruit bat (*payak*, *Ptenochirus jagorii*), palm civet, and civet cat. Young piglet, deer and monkey are captured alive and kept as pets. Birds are sometimes hunted and their eggs collected. While the game animals and mammals in particular are affected by temporary fluctuations in their food supply and by weather conditions (Allen 1985:53–54), the ratio of their exploitation by the Agta varies little across months of a year.

Traditionally, the Agta hunt these game animals with bow (*busog*) and arrow (*pana*). Bows are generally 1.5 m long. The shaft of the bow is made from varieties of palm (e.g., *Livistina* spp.) on which the bowstring of *Ficus* bark (e.g., *dépping*, *kahawad*, or more commonly, nylon) is fastened. This simple type bow can be made by one person in less than two days and can last up to three years.

Many kinds of arrow heads, some game specific, are made by the Agta through "hot smithing." On the basis of their construction and general function, arrows can be divided into nondetachable and detachable types; they can also be divided into barbed or nonbarbed types (see Estioko-Griffin 1984:83–111 for detail description). The shaft is made of *bigiw* (*Miscanthus* sp.) grass. Its anterior end is sharpened and its posterior end fletched with the feathers of birds, particularly the rufous hornbill (*kalaw*, *Buceros* sp.).

According to the informants, the shotgun was introduced to the Agta approximately three generations ago (i.e., the early decades of this century). Later, during World War II, Agta acquired many more firearms from the retreating Japanese soldiers, who were being defeated and killed by the American army. It is said that in the 1960s, the bow and arrow was already being replaced by the shotgun. In 1972, however, when martial law was declared in the Philippines and possession of firearms was made illegal, Agta went back to their dependence on bow and arrow. Today, while the possession of firearms is still illegal, Agta are acquiring them through various sources. Since the shotgun shells are scarce and expensive, Agta resort to repacking the used shells with match heads and scrap lead. While Agta realize that the shotgun has greater firing range than their traditional bow and arrow, they point out certain disadvantages of the shotgun. For example, the bow and arrow allows the hunter to shoot at game successively, a feat not possible with the shotgun. Nonetheless, the shotgun has become a prestige possession particularly among young men and is slowly replacing the bow and arrow.

The Agta have traditionally used dogs for hunting. In the Disabungan area, Agta own approximately three hunting dogs per family. In spite of the fact that dogs are not trained nor are they regularly fed, they are considered valuable possessions. They are most helpful in locating and cornering game and in driving the farrowing sows out of the nest. Good hunting dogs often go out on their own and drive the game back toward the camp for the hunters to corner and kill.

The simple hunting tools, which in themselves contribute to check the depletion ratio of large game animals (see Mudar 1985:79), is compensated by the amazingly varied Agta hunting strategies (see also Estioko-Griffin 1984:146–55). During rainy days, Agta use a searching (*puhab*) strategy in and around the visitation area of game animals. Immediately after the downpour, when fresh animal tracks are visible, a trailing (*tikéd*) strategy is used. However, when it is not raining, these strategies are not effective; the sound (and smell) of the hunter's approach drives the game away. Thus, Agta use three other hunting strategies. The first, called ambushing (*sanéb*), is done by waiting along the game spoor. The second strategy, which is particularly used to kill wild pigs, is hiding (*hos*) and is done by waiting near wallowing and feeding areas. The third strategy is the cornering (*sagide*) of game by dogs and humans.

The Agta used a number of collective hunting techniques in the past. One that is still popular is called *manganop*. It uses the cornering strategy and involves up to 20 people. In this technique dogs are sent to scout the forest slopes. As barking dogs alert people, women and children take positions to help corner the game so that hunters can stalk it. Such expeditions have to be well coordinated by making particular sounds and nonverbal signs. Agta knowledge of the game behavior, familiarity with the locale, and well developed sense of direction in the rain forest, often make such hunting trips successful. During the 64 days of observation, 27% ($N = 51$) of the hunting trips used this collective technique and of them, 40% were successful (see Appendix 7).

Individual hunting techniques differ from collective ones in that the hunters are mostly adult males, and dogs are not used. In the most popular individual hunting technique, called *mangaliduk*, the hunters use searching, trailing, ambushing and hiding strategies depending on the weather conditions. As soon as game is spotted, they tiptoe with their eyes fixed on the game. When they find the game within the shooting range of bow and arrow or shotgun, they shoot it. The Disabungan Agta were using this technique in 59% of the hunting expeditions and the majority (57%) of such individual hunting trips were successful.

"Jacking" (*maglente*) with a flashlight strapped on the hunter's forehead has become a popular hunting strategy, particularly during the new moon period. This technique is also an effective way to kill fruit bats. The Disabungan Agta were observed following this strategy in 14% of their hunting expeditions.

Agta make use of various traps to kill game. For example, pig and deer are caught by using spear traps (viz. *bilatik*, *takdik*, *kalawat*). Trapping is however usually done for secondary game. Python are caught by tying one end of a rattan reed to a tree and another end into a loop to be placed around the mouth of the hole where the python dwells. As the python is teased by throwing rocks, it comes out and gets caught in the loop trap. Simple snares (*sékwat*) are placed on trails to catch wild cats and chickens. Once an animal is caught, the supporting pole of the snare jerks to strangle it. Various other cage traps (*salakumba*), rattan loops (*bélaybay*) or lasso-type ropes (*biklog*) are used for wild chickens and birds. A sticky latex is placed on poles to catch perching birds. Recently, rubber slingshots are also becoming popular in bird hunting.

The Agta hunt frequently. In the 64 days of observation of one band of Disabungan Agta, at least one individual went out to hunt every day over a 41 day period. While the average size of the band was 34 individuals during the observation period, they fielded four people (11%) on an average hunting day. The hunting parties were most commonly formed around sibling, brother-in-law, father-son and husband-wife relationships (see also Estioko-Griffin 1986:138). Agta also prefer to hunt in small parties to avoid noise problems. Thus, while the size of hunting parties varied from one to twelve individuals, 67% of the hunting parties were composed of less than four individuals. A two-person party was most successful in securing game and claimed 36% of all game killed by the band in that period (see Appendix 7). Individuals, too, varied in their frequency of participation in hunting as well as in their success rate. Five adult males repeatedly hunted and the majority of the kills were made by them. Of them, one hunter in particular secured 23% of the total kill. While the most successful hunter brought back three game animals from each of seven hunting trips he made, another male consistently failed to secure any even on his eleventh trip. The band as a whole killed two game animals in every three days. In terms of meat return, one kilogram of meat was acquired in every five person-hours of hunting. If the labor input of only successful hunters are accounted, the same amount of meat was acquired in half the time.

In addition to these numerous strategies and techniques, Agta also resort to various types of rituals to assure their luck in hunting. For example, if a hunter consistently fails to kill a game animal, he goes through a ritual to restore his luck in hunting. In the most common ritual (called *maggilgil*), an individual, usually a female, chews betel nut and spits over the head, body and upper arms of the hapless hunter. In a ritual (called *maghotong*), the unsuccessful hunter collects plants such as *Imparata* and elephant grass, and burns them to inhale the smoke. Similarly, if the hunting dogs consistently fail to corner game or to track down wounded ones, they are made to smell (*magsuub*) the burnt excreta of game animals "in order to sharpen their senses."

The Agta also observe a number of forms of hunting etiquette. For example, it is taboo for the hunter himself to carry undressed game into the camp. He has to enter the camp as unceremoniously as he left. He carries his hunting tool in his right hand or on his shoulder to indicate that he was successful in securing a game. As he is sighted, another band member goes out to carry back (*magsubul*) the undressed game. In the case of wild pig, the skin of the forehead is taken out to be worn as an arm band by the hunter or his close relatives. The hunter keeps the jaw bone (*sélang*) of the game as a trophy.

The hunting emphasis of the Agta of the tropical rain forest, reflected in their elaborate hunting strategies as well as the time allocation and caloric intake, initially came as a surprise (Griffin et al. 1978:43). This was rooted in the two assumptions prevalent among anthropologists in the 1970s. First, based on ethnographic studies, it was believed that foragers of the equatorial zone, including the Asian Negritos, relied on plant food more than on animal food. In fact, it was believed that the majority of the technologically primitive societies outside the arctic and subarctic regions depended more on gathered food than on meat (Lee 1968:42). Second, it was believed that the tropical rain forest was poorer in animal resources, particularly large game, than plant resources. It was realized later that in spite of the high plant biomass, the rain forest environment was poor in human plant foods (Hutterer 1982:134–35, 153). Given the new knowledge, it was logical that the Agta emphasize the hunting subsistence.

One might argue that the Agta reliance on hunting is due to recent lack of emphasis on gathering. There is in fact some evidence that gathering among the Agta has been de-emphasized due to some recent changes. For example, the Agta dependence on outside cereals has led to a decreased degree of reliance on gathering (Allen 1985:56). Gathering of wild plant foods also becomes redundant with the increasing horticultural activity of the Agta groups. Further, wild plant foods are the most seriously affected resources following the recent environmental degradation. But there is evidence to suggest that gathering among the Agta did not play more than a subsidiary role even in the remote past. It has been stated above that tropical rain forests like the one the Agta inhabit provide relatively few plant resources for direct human consumption. While the Agta could have exploited a number of wild starch foods, they could not have primarily depended on them. As we will see shortly, the small inventory of Agta plant foods and simple gathering technology suggest they have never depended heavily on gathering. Agta informants also believe that their forefathers relied on gathering only as a subsidiary foraging activity.

Gathering among the Agta is also not always a purposive activity like hunting but more of an opportunistic activity. Generally, it is either done on an encounter basis or practiced in conjunction with other activities. Because plant resources are more concentrated there, Agta usually gather along the open and shaded stream vegetation areas. As the second most important traditional subsistence activity, the gathering activity takes up 10% of the working time of the Disabungan Agta. Of this time, two-thirds is spent in the collection of wild starch alone (e.g., wild yam, caryota palm pulp, wild banana, and other starchy fruits). In terms of caloric input, the Disabungan Agta derive 16% of their total intake from gathered plant resources. A gathering party is often composed of less than three individuals, usually women and children. A typical trip lasts less than two hours and covers a circuit distance of less than three kilometers.

Today, the Agta exploit a variety of wild yams, which make up the bulk of their uncultivated source of carbohydrate (see also Allen 1985:63). These tubers can be gathered all year but the highest return per unit of labor is gained between August and October when the tubers mature. Thus, just before the northeast monsoon begins, Agta devote much time to harvesting this food source (*magkali*). There are at least six varieties of edible tubers identified by the Agta on the basis of vines and leaves, shallowness of roots, and taste. The most commonly exploited yam is *ilus* (*Dioscorea cf. filiformis*), which has deep roots and is found only along river terraces. A split bamboo (*sugsug*) or knife (*guho*) is used in digging this yam. In an observation period of 32 days, Agta women were gathering one kilogram of yam per hour of work. Other varieties are less common but are sought for their particular tastes. They include bitter yam (*segday*), sticky yam (*balo*) and a yam also eaten by wild pigs (*baay*). Most of the latter varieties of wild tuber occur only in higher elevations. Agta state that occasionally when they get "tired of eating rice," they move their camp upriver to subsist on these wild roots.

The plant food that is consistently mentioned in the Agta folklore is the caryota palm. The palm, which resembles sago palm but provides less starch per tree, is pulped by the Agta to acquire the starch. Its symbolic significance is suggested by its indispensable importance in the traditional Agta wedding feast. It is also considered an ideal gift while visiting kin at distant camps.

According to the Agta informants, the caryota palm (*Caryota cumingii*) reaches flowering age in three to four years. The year following the flowering is the most ideal time to pulp (*magagél*) it, although it can be done with decreasing return for a few more years. There is no particular month to gather this resource; they tend to pulp it during the northeast monsoon when they rely less on cultivated cereals. The pulping of this food is an extremely laborious job. The processing requires continuous soaking and rinsing with water. The pith has to be removed by pounding with a wooden mallet (*pasok*), especially designed for this purpose. Approximately 20 person-hours of work are required to acquire one kilogram of such starch.

Several varieties of wild fruits are opportunistically collected. One of them is a starchy fruit (*bihungay, Diplodicus paniculatus*) which is commonly collected and eaten (see Allen 1985:57); called the "traditional rice" of the Agta, they formerly used this fruit to the same extent that they depend on cultivated rice today (Estioko-Griffin 1984:174). Other wild fruits include guava, wild banana, wild citrus, *pélluat* (*Nephelium lappaceum*), and various palm (e.g., *bisal, sahed*) and rattan (e.g., *sahetsahet*) fruits. Wild vegetables are occasionally collected and they include fern, bitter melon (*parya, Momordica charantia*), wild chili, the heart of several species of palm (e.g., *sakon*) and rattan. Agta also collect honey from three kinds of honey bees (*giyaw, pitukan, palég*), which are found either inside tree trunks or hanging on tree branches. They collect it by locating honey beehives through their observation of the flight of bees (*magtalduk*). Honey can be collected all year around but the period immediately after the peak flowering season (March to May) is the most productive.

The degree of Agta reliance on the various animal and plant foods is little affected by the minor climatic fluctuations of their environment. That is to say that the Agta do not experience "lean season" regarding their traditional animal or plant food sources. While specific wild foods are exploited more successfully during particular months of the year (e.g., wild yam from August to October), the percentage of caloric contribution from the wild animal as well as plant resources varies little as they continuously have access to other similar food resources (see Allen 1985; Estioko-Griffin 1986:169,

194 for similar data). As we shall see later, external trade is disrupted by the monsoon floods, which affects the Agta reliance on wild food resources.

The small climatic variation, particularly the northeast monsoon floods, has, however, an effect on the Agta exploitation of aquatic resources. Because of the continuous rain, floods are common in this season. In addition, the diurnal temperature varies so that early mornings and late evenings can be cold. Thus, Agta prefer to fish only infrequently. It is in this sense that fishing to the Agta is a seasonal economic pursuit.

Of the number of fresh water fauna in the rivers of the valley watershed of the Sierra Madre, the most preferred and sought after is the eel (*Anguilla* sp.). In these rivers, Agta also exploit the seven most common species of fish. In the order of their exploitation, they are *kulapia*, *pelléng*, *délag*, *buhase*, *banug*, *mudi*, and *ludung*. In addition, a single variety of river shrimp, crab and aquatic frog as well as three varieties of fresh water shellfish (*pisepis*, *guhong*, *sukkul*) are collected. Agta also claim occasionally to kill and eat crocodiles which are found particularly in coastal river mouths.

The fishing gear of the Agta is composed of a few simple tools. The most basic one is an iron rod (*bakal*) with a sharpened tip. A rubber band is fastened to its posterior end, which ejects the iron rod to shoot in a slingshot fashion. Sometimes the rod is mounted on a gun-like wooden body to trigger it. A miniature barbed arrow (*béttik*) can also be attached by a string to the rod to kill eel or larger species of fish. Hunting bow and arrow can also be used to fish by standing on the banks of large rivers or the edges of open sea during low tides. Agta say that their deep pond and open sea fishing techniques have been greatly aided by the introduction of fishing goggles by the Japanese lumbermen early in this century. These days, such goggles are locally made by a few skilled Agta. Many coastal Agta groups, particularly those who have ready access to reef or lagoon environment, have begun to use line fishing and net fishing techniques (Estioko-Griffin 1984:43).

The simple fishing tools of the Agta are balanced by the sophisticated and varied strategies and techniques employed in using them (see Bennagen 1976:12–13). Agta informants report that the aquatic fauna can be categorized into "those that can smell humans" (e.g., *banug*, *buhase*, *ludung*) and others that cannot. Eel in particular is said not only to be sensitive to smell but also to have the power to hear human voices. Agta claim that the appropriate technique of fishing is determined by the category of the prey.

The most common technique of Agta fishing is pond fishing (*magléddép*). An individual or a small number of people wear fishing goggles and dive in ponds to shoot fish with the iron slingshot. They chew tobacco "to heat their body" prior to diving if the water is cold. This technique is most effective for killing small fish that cannot smell humans. Shallow fishing (*magpelléng*), is done by standing in shallow water and dipping one's head in water to shoot fish. Bait fishing is done by inserting bait impaled on a wooden stick inside underwater rock shelters. Arrow fishing (*magbéttik*), which requires diving into the pond and shooting the fish with a miniature arrow tip, is effective in killing eel and other larger varieties of fish. The Agta also carry out two variations of night fishing. The first technique is light fishing (*magsulo*), where Agta dive into the ponds with goggles and flashlights strapped to their foreheads. To kill fish which they believe are sensitive to human odor, Agta use another technique (called *magmilik*): roasting small fish and putting them in water to attract fish and eel which are then shot with the iron rod.

Less often Agta participate in collective fishing. Three techniques in particular are employed. Poison fishing (*magtube*) uses the croton oil plant (*Croton tigilum*) and other plants (e.g., *sagisa*, *mubli*, *tayadan*) as poison. The bark of these plants is pounded and left to soak in two to three subsequent places in small rivers. These poisons effectively kill some fish and stun others. Today commercial poison, particularly sodium cynide balls, are used to drug the fish. The second technique of collective fishing is rattan fishing (*magsahet*). A long rattan frame strung with stone weights is carried along the river to drive the fish as people wait at a specific location to shoot them. The third collective technique (called *magkalwang*) is done by diverting the stream whereby fish in this shallow water are easily caught.

In spite of these numerous techniques, fishing is only a tertiary economic activity among the valley watershed Agta groups. The Disbungan Agta, who do not have ready access to open sea, devote only 4% of their working time to river fishing. The return, hour for hour, from fishing is equally insignificant. An observation among one band showed that Agta spend, on average, four person-hours of work to procure one kilogram of aquatic protein. For the same group, fishing provided only 2% of their total caloric intake (see Appendix 10). The Agta of the coastal watershed however devote more time and get a better return from fishing; they fish many more varieties of fresh water and marine resources including lobster, mollusk, sea turtle and octopus (Estioko-Griffin 1984:44–46).

The Old Rules

The foraging strategies of the Agta are effective means for subsisting in a rain forest environment. Nonetheless, the Agta individuals or families can experience fluctuations in the procurement of specific resources over time. This creates short-term uncertainties for the Agta in their day-to-day living. Such uncertainties are negotiated by the Agta with a flexible sociocultural mechanisms (often called the "Old Rules"). In particular, there are three such adaptive mechanisms among the Agta, namely the division of labor, sharing, and flux.

The sexual division of labor among the Agta is flexible and nonprohibitive. There is no work activity which physically requires exclusion of one sex. While usually only men make bows and arrows and usually only women build lean-tos, these activities can be participated in by either sex. Further, the images of man as hunter and woman as gatherer, popular among hunter-gatherer specialists, does not seem to apply to the Agta. Researchers have found that women among a particular group of Agta, the southeast Cagayan group, are successful bow and arrow hunters of large game (Estioko-Griffin 1985; Goodman et al. 1985). Among the Disabungan Agta, as among other groups, while women only occasionally hunt with bow and arrow, their participation in hunting is very common; women without males accompanying them sometimes hunt pig or deer with dogs and machetes. Statistically, 14 of every 100 hunters are women (see Appendix 7), and women spend one-third of their foraging time in hunting-related activities (see Appendix 6). To the Agta, differences in the male-female roles are seen only in the varying degree of their participation in specific activities. For example, while males spend 75% of their working time hunting, females spend only 8% of their working time in this activity. Men spend an average of 4.5 hours every day in direct food production and processing activities (namely hunting, gathering, fishing, trading and swiddening) as opposed to women who devote only 1.6 hours to such activities (see Appendix 5).

There are also no age-specific activities among the Agta. The *degree* of participation by an individual in specific activities, however, varies depending on the age and marital status of the individual. Among a band of Disabungan Agta, married adults in general spend 3 hours every day in food production (foraging or otherwise) activities, while unmarried young adults (age 9 and above) contribute only 2.5 hours. Among men, married adults put in the most time (5.1 hours) per day, while boys spend 2.7 hours. In the case of females, it is the reverse. While married women who must shoulder major child-care responsibility devote the least time (1.2 hours) to direct food production activities, young unmarried girls contribute twice the time (2.4 hours, see Appendix 5). Paradoxically, however, married women, who contribute the least hours to food production also carry out the most diversified activities such as gathering, fishing, hunting, trading, and swiddening, as well as child-care, household chores, and house construction. Married men, who devote the maximum hours everyday, do so mostly in a few activities. This flexible division of labor is an Agta response to make efficient use of the available human energy and to offset the limits imposed by the technology.

While it might seem that an obvious strategy to circumvent the short-term uncertainties would be the storing of food surplus for future consumption, unfortunately, effective food storage for a longer period requires two prerequisites. Proper climatic conditions (e.g., artic) must exist, and there must be an abundance of resources. For the Agta, the high humidity and temperature of their tropical equatorial environment run counter to conditions required in long-term storing of food. Second, in terms of general resource availability, there is no marked abundance of specific resources. It is therefore an imperative for the Agta to depend on regular foraging; they must procure the necessary resources every day, or at least every few days.

The Agta have, however, two specific sociocultural mechanisms to help solve their problem of short-term uncertainty in resource procurement. One is the strategy of food sharing, and the other, *flux*, a term that describes both the changes in band membership and shifting location of camp sites.

Found in varying degrees in all hunter-gatherer societies, sharing is the popular means to allocate the available resources. Sahlins, who coined the term *generalized reciprocity* for sharing, defines it as "transactions that are putatively altruistic, transactions on the line of assistance given and if possible and necessary, assistance returned" (1965:147). That is, sharing is altruistic and based on generosity and other moral sanctions.

Sharing (*bahagi*) among the Agta is an economic exchange of procured wild resources. The unit participating in this economic exchange is the household and not the individual; irrespective of family size or the food situation, each household gets one share of the food. Sharing can involve simultaneous exchange of the same food between households. It is also a social exchange among the Agta since it generally follows the idiom of kinship (e.g., Service 1966:17) and residence. It is altruistic in the sense that the return is not expected by a specific time or in a specific form. It is informal; no one asks for or rejects a share, nor are they openly thankful for it. While it was earlier reported that sharing among the Agta is regulated by ritual (Peterson 1978a:18, 39, 84, 102), Agta informants deny that there are any jural or ritual sanctions in their practice of sharing. What is seen is that those households who deliberately violate the rules of sharing are privately criticized and occasionally left out of future sharing, and those who fail to reciprocate, for instance, due to sickness, privately express their shame (*sanike*).

The practice of food sharing among the Agta is also determined by the type of food being shared. The meat of wild animals is the most preferred food of the Agta, followed by aquatic protein and finally by plant foods. Given this general framework, the higher the ranking of the wild food item, the more frequent is its sharing. With the exception of birds, the meat of all game is almost always shared (e.g., Woodburn 1980:801). As soon as the game is quartered, the hunter's family sets aside a portion to be traded, and the remaining portion is meticulously weighed to insure equal share among families. Eel and fish are shared but not equally. Gathered foods are shared only among families who are present at the time of consumption. Tools such as bow and arrow, shotgun, and hunting dog, as well as clothes and utensils may also be similarly shared.

The degree of extra-household sharing is partly determined by the kinship network. The rule is that the closer the kin relationship between families, the more intense is the sharing. For example, fish and plant foods are more frequently shared among close kin than distant kin. Close lineal kin share even cooked food either by cooking as a group, by offering a plateful of food to another, or by movement of individuals to each other's kitchens. However, as all families of a band are in a serially related kinship network, ultimately foods get equally distributed among families, particularly foods of the higher categories. Appendix 11 reflects this fact as all four family units of a Disabungan Agta band showed similar energy intakes.

Residence contiguity is another factor that affects the food sharing among the Agta. As a general rule, sharing within a camp is more intense; it is only occasionally that sharing takes place across camps, and most often only meat is shared in this case. For example, if two camps are closely located, meat is divided by camps (*tolbék*), irrespective of band size. While scarce goods such as salt, tobacco and rice also are shared on request, fish and vegetables are rarely shared.

Through sharing, the Agta maintain a regular distribution of food resources between and among families. In other words, the sharing of food produces what Nietschmann (1973:211) calls a "latent food cache." Sharing among the Agta is a built-in mechanism to offset the short-term fluctuations of particular food resources (see also Weissner 1977:11–12).

The practice of sharing may also have other functions. For example, Lee has suggested that sharing among foragers is a mechanism for meeting the physiological needs of individual members (1969:74). Though sharing results in nutritional benefits by insuring that food resources are distributed, as Speth (n.d.a: 2) has suggested, this does not mean that individual members get equal portions. In the case of the Agta, where the family, and not the individual, is the unit of sharing, individuals across families receive unequal shares. Members within a family may receive unequal individual shares due to their presence or absence at the meal time, or to all members dining together from one single utensil.

Sharing is perhaps a mechanism to insure efficient consumption and thus, metabolism of food items. Without the practice of sharing, individual families among the foraging Agta could end up with an erratic surfeit of certain foods and a scarcity of other foods. Considering that the Agta cannot effectively store these surfeits, at times they would have to consume in large quantities. Other consequences aside, such single large consumption of food would result in a regular physiological waste as part of the amount consumed would not be metabolized (McArthur 1974:114). Through sharing, such surfeits get distributed among families (and bands) and the physiological waste is minimized. This hypothesis gets support from the fact that meat is an item that is in frequent surfeit among the Agta hunter-gatherers and an item most regularly shared. It is recognized that protein, the main source of which is meat, if taken in excess of what the body can use, must be catabolized. The sharing of meat is thus physiologically more efficient as it assures a small but regular intake of protein by individuals.

While they may be aware of some of the above-listed functions, the Agta do not practice sharing for those specific reasons. To them, sharing is an exchange of food among closely related (or residing) families and a means to counter the pattern of daily fluctuations in food procurement.

The Agta also use another sociocultural mechanism called flux to meet the demands imposed by short-term fluctuations of food resources. Flux is defined here as frequent shifts of camp sites and the changeover of members between bands. The pattern of flux among the Agta is based on two important principles—camp movement and fluid band composition—described in the following pages.

Camp movement is the collective move of a band to a new campsite. In sharing, resources are "moved" between people; in camp movement, it is people who move between resources (Cashdan 1980:718). Thus, the nature of the distribution of resources influences the camp movement. It was mentioned above that every watershed area, and often individual river valleys, of the Agta rain forest can provide most of the important traditional resources, but no area is abundant in particular resources. The nearby resources quickly become scarcer within a few weeks of exploitation, and have to be acquired by making extended trips. To lower the energy cost, Agta bands move to another area, which again provides most of these resources. It is for this reason that the Agta use camp movement as a "mapping on" strategy for resource exploitation (Binford 1980:12, 14) and as a cultural mechanism to offset the limits of their physical environment (Turnbull 1968:137).

Frequency as well as distance travelled are important dimensions of camp movement. The ethnographic data indicate that the rain forest hunter-gatherers, while maintaining high residence mobility, have shorter intercamp distances and annual circuit distances than desert groups (see Binford 1980:7). Most Agta groups are fully nomadic in that they practice frequent camp movement (see Murdock 1967:159). With the exception of two months during the peak northeast monsoon, when bands tend to prolong their stays in one campsite, camp movement is frequent: one band of the Disabungan Agta were observed making 20 residential moves during one annual cycle. While the length of stay in one campsite varied from less than a week to two months (during the northeast monsoon), on an average the band moved every 18 days. The distance covered in such camp movement was small. The Disabungan Agta band travelled a mean distance of 5 kilometers between camps and their total annual circuit distance was 107 kilometers.

Discussions among the Agta pertaining to camp movement (*kobu*) are more frequent than the moves. One family initiates the discussion by passing the word to others informally. Informally again, the families that agree with the idea support it by emphasizing the disadvantages of their present campsite and idealizing the proposed campsite. The Agta camp movement is crucial for gathering and to some extent for fishing, as well as for trade. Arguments for or against such moves will revolve around these topics. Because hunting depends on mobile animals, it is not an important consideration. Men and women freely voice their opinion on residence change, but women, who must carry out the most gathering, have the final say. The fact that some members argue against such moves also indicates that Agta are changing their campsites before the local resources completely run out. Frequent camp movements are thus part of a mechanism to check the over-exploitation of resources.

Unless the residential move is culturally prescribed (e.g., death of a band member), the decision for such a move is rarely unanimous. Only after a prolonged period of confusion does the majority opinion prevail. Once the decision to move camp is finalized, the day or time of the projected move sets off another episode of confusion. While Agta families have few belongings to transport, the argument over who should carry them can delay the move. Still resentful of the decision, some members complain about rain or sun to delay the move. It may take hours to several days to make the final move. Occasionally, the decision is reversed at the final moment or even after some families have already left for the new camp. The travel is leisurely unless a game animal is encountered to provoke a hunting spree. Frequent stops are made to chew betel nut, fish, gather or cook and even to take a nap. Once the destination is reached, the families either claim their old lean-tos or build new ones.

While, on the one hand, the precise reasons and schedules of Agta camp movement are dependent on multiple factors, the sites and thus the distances involved in such moves are predictable to the Agta themselves. As mentioned above, the Agta bands use only a limited number of campsites. Each such site is scrutinized depending on the other determining factors (e.g., trading convenience or weather). The trails between such campsites are generally agreed upon.

The band-level residential mobility of the Agta is a response to environmental constraints, but there is another aspect of the Agta flux that is not motivated by economic considerations (see Turnbull 1965; Lee 1972b; Woodburn 1968a; Silberbauer 1972). *Fluid band composition* is defined here as the changeover of residences by individual families.

The Agta prefer to maintain an optimum band size of three to five families. However, intermittent temporary fluctuations in band size do occur. Agta families do change their residence temporarily: an Agta household may decide to leave the wife's kin and reside temporarily with the husband's kin; a family might visit a distant camp to seek shamanistic services; or a new marital alliance or death of a member may bring changes in the kinship network and thus a change in residence. A few ceremonial occasions may call for temporary fusion of a few bands. During the course of six months, one band of the Disabungan Agta was observed to vary from two to seventeen families. However, it must be emphasized that these fluctuations are always temporary in nature. Any such significant deviation from the modal band size triggers the process of either fusion (*magpisan*) or fission (*maghiwalay*) of families so that the ideal band size is attained. Once this is achieved, Agta tend to discourage band fluidity. Consequently, the Agta remain a low valency society, experiencing low degrees of band fluidity.

The above analysis of Agta band fluidity suggests that its major function is to reconcile social obligations. This view is contrary to Peterson's suggestion that it is the Agta mechanism to distribute individual members relative to resources (1978a:21). It also runs counter to the idea that fluid band composition is a major conflict-resolving mechanism among hunter-gatherers (see Lee and DeVore 1968:9, 156; for a similar argument on the Agta, see Peterson 1978a:74). Turnbull, who claims that the function of fluid band composition is political adaptation, puts it more succinctly when he says that the processes of fission and fusion follow "lines of dissent rather than those of descent" (1968:137). For the Agta, though, this is not true. Their band fluidity follows the line of kinship.

The egalitarian character of the Agta economy is facilitative rather than competitive (see Silberbauer 1981:249); the families in a band do not have to compete over resources because they share the procured resources. Given these conditions, there is an atmosphere of noncompetition with regard to resources use. Dissent among kin, whenever it arises, is easily forgiven or forgotten. Non-kin, on the other hand, distrust each other and are often involved in disputes of varying degrees of intensity. Thus, dissent among the Agta is more frequent as the distance in genealogical relationship increases. Such dissent among band members who are not directly closely related may create factions and the ultimate fission of the band along the line of kinship; it is also for this reason that the Agta themselves can predict the lines of band fission and fusion. One can, therefore, conclude that the fluid band composition of the Agta is due to kinship rather than dissent *per se*.

7
The Social Circumscription

The Agta population of Isabela is divided into four linguistic groups. Members of one linguistic group maintain not only economic but also social and political isolation from their counterparts. In this chapter, this sociopolitical isolation will be examined. It will be argued that an Agta linguistic group is not a "territorial" group as it neither owns an exclusive territory nor exercises exclusive rights over resources (see also Griffin 1984:106). It maintains its sociopolitical isolation simply because its kinship network does not extend beyond its linguistic group, and in the absence of such kinship network, the Agta do not interact.

Pattern of Interaction

It was described above that watershed groups, the units within a linguistic group, maintain economic independence from each other. The watershed groups maintain this independence partly because of the rugged ridge of the Sierra Madre and the great physical distance that would be involved in any regular economic exchanges. Economic independence is also maintained because the two watershed areas are ecologically similar with respect to the traditional resources of the Agta. These two reasons aside, there are no cultural or other sanctions prohibiting the watershed groups within a linguistic group from entering economic exchanges. Moreover, any Agta individual, family or band may take up residence in any site and may exploit resources from any place within the linguistic area.

Such a description of the Agta watershed groups stands, however, in sharp contradiction with one earlier published report. Regarding a single watershed group who are part of what I call the Palanan-Divilacan linguistic group, J. Peterson writes:

> The Agta recognize three territories within Palanan ... While all share resources in common, each is characterized by variation in the availability of these resources. The areal

> variation in resources affects Agta subsistence within each territory, [and] relations among Agta in different territories . . . [1978a:6].
>
> . . . territories are clearly bounded and rules governing access to resources within a territory are widely accepted . . . territorial rights are preserved by threat of death to violators . . . Should trespass occur, any individual from that territory may kill the trespasser . . . [ibid.:25].
>
> . . . the three territories seasonally experience differential resource potential . . . the Agta meet daily fluctuations in food supply by maintaining flexibility in economic behavior . . . This economic adaptation, however, does not necessarily assure survival during seasonal fluctuations of food supply, catastrophic occurrences such as typhoons, or other events which might affect food supply over longer periods of time [ibid.:45].
>
> . . . much of the flexibility of Agta resource exploitation hinges on successful marriages, especially territorially exogamous marriages [ibid.:14].

In the following pages, I will provide data to show that the Agta groups (linguistic, watershed, or river valley) do not see themselves as owning or controlling their resources. There are few areal and seasonal variations of the Agta resources. Territorial exogamy described by Peterson (1978a) is only a regular marriage relationship among members of a linguistic group.

Territoriality, in the sense that this term is conventionally understood, means territorial ownership and control. Territoriality is a pattern of behavior which results in competition between members of a species for space (Odum 1975:129). Earlier ethnographic studies on hunter-gatherers reported that territorial behavior was common among these societies (e.g., Radcliffe-Brown 1931; 1952:33–34). Later studies, however, showed that the hunter-gatherers neither exclusively occupy a territory nor defend it (Hiatt 1968:101). Summarizing the hunter-gatherer literature, Lee and DeVore write that these societies are not characterized by corporate ownership of property (1968:8–9). Woodburn claims that among all hunter-gatherers, territories, if defined at all, do not substantially constrain individual choice of residence or use of resources (1980:795). For particular desert hunter-gatherers, Silberbauer writes that militant territorialism would be an ecological luxury that they could ill afford (1981:185–87). In short, the evidence suggests that territoriality among hunter-gatherers is perhaps a fallacy (N. Peterson 1979:111, 125).

Let us examine the Agta case. The Agta do not form corporate groups that exercise communal rights over persons and property (see Murdock 1960:4). They thus lack any stipulations regarding land and resource ownership. Moreover, the Agta rain forest homeland does not experience many regional variations or localizations in plant or animal resources. The three territories of the Agta claimed by Peterson (1978a) are actually part of a single coastal rain forest chain interrupted only by rivers. Because all three areas are located within a small perimeter of the Palanan Bay area, they should exhibit a very similar diversity in plant and animal species. All three areas have access to a similar nexus of resources including those from estuarine, lagoon, reef or open sea areas.

Interwoven with the argument of areal variation is Peterson's suggestion that her three territories also experience seasonal variations in resources. I have argued above that this part of northeastern Luzon experiences no true ecological seasonality.[1] The nonseasonal conditions tend to maintain the similar structure and composition of the local rain forest vegetation throughout the year (Wernstedt and Spencer 1967:62; see also Myers 1980; Allen 1985; Marten 1984). Consequently, as opposed to Peterson's claim, there is no marked seasonal fluctuation of the traditional Agta resources. Since there is year-round availability of the Agta resources in sufficient proportion and quantity and since the Agta depend on a nexus of animal, plant and aquatic resources at any period of a year, they do not experience seasonal stress and scarcity in forest food resources.

The tropical environment of the Agta is not like the arid environment where certain resources (e.g., water) are limiting factors, and where the possibility of extreme conditions prevails (see Silberbauer 1981:288–89). Nonetheless, natural catastrophes such as typhoons can bring short-term fluctuations in specific Agta natural resources (Griffin 1984:110; Allen 1985:54). For example, when the typhoon disturbs the flowering of the dipterocarp, it may not bear fruit, which are eaten by the Agta game animals. But because the path of a typhoon is wide enough to affect all the Agta areas (such as the Palanan Bay) equally, Agta would find no insurance in the resources of another territory. Given the absence of any significant variations of resources, Agta neither need to exploit resources from another area nor defend their own.

In a logical sequence to the claim that Agta face regional and seasonal fluctuations in resources, Peterson advances the thesis that they must have access to extra-territorial resources to assure their survival. According to her, this is achieved by a conscious practice of territorially exogamous marriages; that is, parents encourage or even dictate the marriage of their children with individuals from another territory in order to gain access to resources there. Headland (1978:129–33) has questioned most of this ethnographic data presented by Peterson. For example, while Peterson asserts that access to resources is explicitly discussed during matrimonial arrangements, Headland claims that this is never the case. According to Peterson, circumcision is performed by a father to obligate and dictate his son's marriage, but Headland reports that if it is done, it is always done without the knowledge and participation of the father. I have discussed above how marriage among the Agta, instead of being premeditated by families to gain access to resources in other areas, is very much an individual, social arrangement in the sense that as long as the individual abides by the Agta incest rule, he or she is free to marry any person from anywhere within the linguistic area. Because close residence also often means close kinship ties, one is normally required to marry an individual from a distant camp. Thus, what Peterson calls territorial exogamy is simply the inevitable Agta marital arrangement resulting from a high degree of kin relatedness within band, river valley and watershed groups, and the incest rule prohibiting kin marriages.

To return to the topic of the Agta linguistic groups, these groups, composed of the watershed groups, which interact through kinship, marriage and, if and when such need arises, through residence relocation and exploitation of resources from the same area, form the Agta social units. The Agta members interact within the linguistic group (depending on their degree of kinship) and between linguistic groups there is marked social isolation. There is little or no kin relationship between linguistic groups; neither is there trade, other material exchange or information flow. An Agta band living at one end of the linguistic area can have information about their sister bands who live three days' walk away, but not of bands of different linguistic group who may live only a day away. An analysis shows that these linguistic groups share 80–87% common vocabularies with one another (see Appendix 3). The absence of any trophic and nontrophic exchanges across linguistic groups results in minimal interaction. Following the social isolation between members of different linguistic groups, a linguistic group maintains a separate homeland area within the Agta forest chain.

As mentioned above, the Agta themselves identify four such linguistic groups[2] in Isabela. Since the area of each linguistic group usually extends across the valley and coastal watersheds, the Agta linguistic groups occupy successive and roughly rectangular areas along the north-south axis of the Sierra Madre range (see Map 2). The Disabungan-Dipagsénghan linguistic group, of which the Disabungan Agta are part, live in three municipalities of the southern half of the Isabela province. Numbering 377, they represent the second largest Agta group in Isabela with their heavy concentration (63.4%) on the interior slopes of the coastal watershed (see Appendix 2). The second linguistic group, the Ilagin-Dikaméy, live in an area to the south of the Disabungan-Dipagsénghan. Concentrated in two municipalities, this is the linguistic group in Isabela which occupies a large part of the valley watershed but does not occupy areas of the coastal watershed. Today, this group also represents the smallest linguistic group (149 people) in Isabela. To the north of the Disabungan-Dipagsénghan lives the largest (856 people) linguistic group, the Palanan-Divilacan. The majority (91%) live in the coastal watershed (and occupy almost three-fifths of the coastal watershed area of Isabela), and the remaining population lives in a narrow corridor in the valley watershed. The northernmost linguistic group in Isabela is the Maconacon-Abuan (also called the southeast Cagayan Agta); a large number of people from this linguistic group also inhabit areas beyond the Isabela-Cagayan provincial boundary. Excluding members who live outside the Isa-

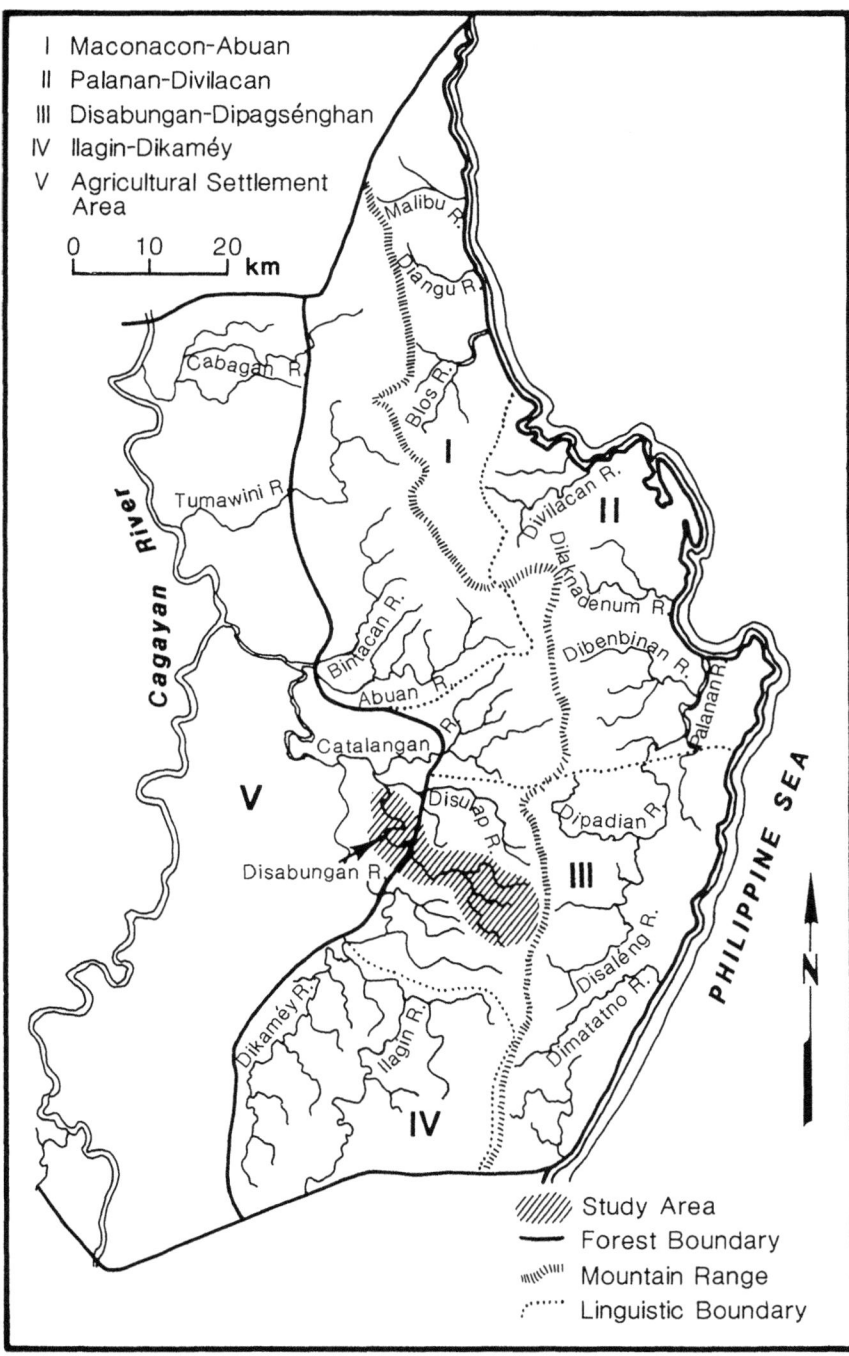

MAP 2. Homeland areas of the Agta linguistic groups in Isabela.

bela province, this group numbers 262 people and represents the third largest linguistic group in Isabela.

Why do linguistic groups maintain social distance from one another? The answer has already been partly provided. There is little or no kin relationship between members of different linguistic groups. Thus, to the Agta, members of another linguistic group are non-kin. From the Agta perspective, non-kin, particularly from another linguistic group, are perceived as untrustworthy, unpredictable and often violence-prone. In Silberbauer's term, they fall beyond the "safety threshold" (1981:62–63) of social interaction. Since any interaction with such people may potentially involve threat and danger, Agta members from different linguistic groups maintain social distance with one another.

Such a negative perception of members of another linguistic group is not totally an unfounded paranoia, but deeply rooted in the long Agta history of interlinguistic raids. The available evidence suggests that organized warfare, in the sense of socially sanctioned and bilaterally agreed upon armed combat, did not exist among the Agta. Instead, the Agta carried out punitive raids (*ngayaw*) which were unilaterally initiated surprise attacks on bands of extralinguistic group. From the informants' stories, it appears that the Agta raids were largely carried out as part of a counter-raiding cycle to avenge standing historical grievances. They neither involved extraction of resources nor taking of slaves and women.

According to Agta informants, the raiding was generally carried out in a long-distance expedition. The raiding party was often composed of closely related able-bodied males numbering five to ten individuals. The most ideal raiding season was from March to May, when floods did not hinder cross-country travel and the abundance of honey solved the food problem for the raiding party. Traditionally, bow and arrow were used in raiding. Allegedly, some groups of Agta raiders also used poison arrows.

For strategic reasons, the raiders preferred to attack on nights between the new moon and the full moon. They approached the enemy camp by moonlight and waited for the darkness to begin the attack. As a designated member from the raiding party signalled (by making a grunting sound), others tiptoed to get closer to the camp. They toppled the lean-tos to trap sleeping families and killed or wounded unsparingly as many people as they could. If they had time, they disfigured bodies of the victims. Occasionally, the raiders took utensils, knives, blankets, bows and arrows, and burned down the lean-tos.

Analyzing the details, it seems that Agta bands experienced either serious threat or actual attack only infrequently—every three to four years, and often casualties were limited to injuries. However, the possibility of raiding was always there and the Agta bands from different linguistic groups remained potential enemies (see Griffin 1984:106; Headland 1986:385). Since there was no truce, Agta always lived with suspicion about outsiders. In such a situation, the only defense the Agta had was to live in a sizable band and to move camp covertly (*maghenhen*) when such threats occurred.

The widespread acquisition of shotguns by Agta groups during World War II brought an interesting turn in the history of the intra-Agta raiding. In the years immediately succeeding the war, the raiding was intensified; one band of Disabungan Agta was raided twice in the same year by raiders from two different linguistic groups. As the use of shotguns became frequent, the casualties rose, not only among people who were attacked, but also among the attackers, for retribution was easy. This eventually served as a deterrent to frequent raiding. Following the declaration of martial law in 1972, when the military confiscated firearms and bows and arrows, the Agta seriously feared that raiding would intensify. Suspicion rose high as both the military and the insurgents recruited different groups of Agta to act as porters, guides and hunters, and mounted expeditions that occasionally resulted in Agta casualties. While the allegations continue, the active practice of raiding has declined among the Isabela Agta. Nonetheless, its long history has left a lasting fear in the minds of the Agta and they therefore believe that the interlinguistic social isolation must remain enforced.

The Agta keep their interlinguistic social distance also by mutual stereotyping and by ethnocentrically contrasting themselves with the other groups. The members of one's own linguistic group are considered true Agta and others are considered to represent deviations; they are either "settled" or, if obviously otherwise, "wild" Agta.

The so-called settled Agta groups are ridiculed by their more traditional counterparts for being servants to the agricultural population. They are thus said to devote little time to hunting, fishing or to the collection of wild foods but live by scavenging agricultural settlements for food. Though most Agta drink, the "settled" Agta are particularly accused of being alcoholics as well as compulsive gamblers. They also are accused of tolerating illicit sexual liaisons between their women and outsiders and thus giving birth to hybrid (*mestiso*) children. In short, such groups are said to have ceased to be Agta and have, therefore, fallen into the non-Agta ranks.

Those groups of Agta who usually fall in the category of settled admit that they have changed. However, they might emphatically deny the accusations directed at them. For one, they claim that they are not yet fully settled. Their forest orientation is decreasing but they still depend on wild resources and possess the technology to exploit them. They are less successful only because wild game and other resources are said to be less abundant where they live today. Sporadically, a small number of women from these groups have married outsiders but widespread illicit sexual relations are denied.

The outside agricultural people also distinguish the settled Agta from others. Because these more acculturated groups have historically lived in and around coastal areas, they are called *dumagat*, literally meaning "people of the sea." But since the Isabela Agta in all probability did not have any traditional maritime technology such as boats, and did not fish in the deep sea, *dumagat* is not a very meaningful term. The Agta do not use this word to describe any of their people, or if they do, it has no connotations of settled vs. unsettled.

The term used by the Agta themselves to describe the less acculturated Agta groups is *ebukid*. This word carries at least three components of meanings. Denotatively, it means "people from the mountain" or groups living in the interior and thus away from agricultural settlements. Because of their distance from agricultural settlements, they have a less intensive interaction with the non-Agta population and have tended to remain more traditional. Due to this, the connotative meaning of the word *ebukid* is "people who are traditional." Often, this word is also used to describe groups who are said to practice active raiding. *Ebukid*, therefore, has a slightly pejorative connotation. In general, Agta see their *ebukid* neighbors as subsisting only on meat and wild roots. The *ebukid* are ridiculed for continuing the traditional Agta customs such as teeth filing, scarification of the body and shaving the pig tail area. Boys do not want to marry girls from such groups, for these groups are said to demand a long and difficult bride service. Such ethnocentrism among Agta linguistic groups provides an excuse for maintaining sociopolitical isolation.

One way the Agta linguistic groups can break their social barriers is through cross-linguistic marriage. While it occurred only rarely in the past, today interlinguistic marriage does occur (see Headland 1986:371, 525), particularly where remarriage of a widow is concerned. Of the 29 currently married couples in the Disabungan area, five cases involved such cross-linguistic marriages and three of them were widow remarriages. The Ilagin-Dikaméy group, which is the smallest in Isabela and constantly faces difficulty in arranging marriages within the group, is said to promote cross-linguistic marriages more aggressively. Such interlinguistic marriages connect two or more linguistic groups through kinship and help ease the open distrust. But again, these marriages entail other problems. For example, linguistic groups differ in their sociocultural rules of bride service (and bride price) and such misunderstandings bring to surface renewed suspicion between members of different linguistic groups. Because a strong undercurrent of distrust prevails between linguistic groups, only those people who are related to both sides and those escorted by them travel across linguistic areas. Ultimately, the fragile alliance due to cross-linguistic marriages remains provisional and the linguistic groups continue to maintain social distance from one another.

To conclude the analysis of the Agta traditional world, it can be said that the relationship between the rain forest environment and the Agta social groupings, defined by kinship and residence pattern, are mediated by their

The Social Circumscription

simple technology and flexible social organization. The Agta linguistic groups themselves maintain sociopolitical isolation from one another because of the absence of interlinguistic kinship networks and the consequent distrust. These socially isolated linguistic groups living in adjacent areas of a single forest chain of northeastern Luzon loosely represent the larger regional population of the Agta. The traditional way of this Agta population is distinctly dominated by three characteristics, namely, the forest orientation, their socioeconomic egalitarianism and mobility.

PART III

THE TRANSITIONAL WORLD

8
The Changes

The preceding part of this study described the morphostatic aspects of the Agta world. It emphasized the systemic relationships of the natural and sociocultural environments that were important in maintaining a traditional Agta way of life. This section will emphasize the morphogenetic aspects. The factors and processes that bring about changes in the structure and organization of the traditional Agta world will be examined here.

The complex process of change in a human society can be completely explained only by analyzing all aspects of the society under question, a cumbersome, if not impossible, task. We are thus forced to focus only on those conditions which have been most radically altered and which are primarily responsible for bringing about change in that human society. Here I will analyze particular altered conditions in the internal Agta system, then describe how the external systems have determined the degree and nature of change among the Agta.

Internal Conditions

One of the most frequently reported modern changes among technologically simple societies is their internal population growth. The analysis of the internal Agta population growth, however, faces problems as there is little historical demographic data on the group. Information on the demographic conditions in the recent past is also sketchy at best and any attempt to expand it creates a number of problems (e.g., Howell 1976, 1980; Harpending 1976; Neel and Chagnon 1968). For reasons mentioned above, the Agta informants cannot provide us with data to analyze their genealogical demography. In addition to the fact that Agta do not know their absolute age, Agta can relate their births only to a few known local historical events. The past Agta population trend therefore must be described indirectly by analyzing their population control mechanisms.

The Agta have few if any cultural means of controlling their fertility. A study on the reproductive behavior of Agta women shows that menarche takes place at a mean age of 17 and menopause at an average age of 44 (Goodman et al. 1985:149, 156). Agta women marry early, at least by 18 years of age (Headland 1986:154), and thus they do not postpone marriage, which could have controlled fertility. Few women remain unmarried, and most widows or divorcees, particularly of the reproductive age, remain single for only a short time. These women bear children early at a mean age of 20 (Goodman et al. 1985:149). Venereal diseases, which can cause pathological sterility, are uncommon. Agta claim not to practice periodic sexual abstinence. They claim to have a knowledge of herbal contraceptives, but their effectiveness in preventing pregnancies, causing abortions or sterility could not be ascertained (Estioko-Griffin 1986:29).

In the absence of any effective physical or cultural restraints on the Agta fertility behavior, one would expect a very high fertility rate. The reproductive studies of the present day Agta population show that, in relative terms, this is true. Goodman et al. (1985) report that the southeast Cagayan Agta women, in comparison to other contemporary foragers, have a longer reproductive period (average 26.8 years), shorter spacing between live births (average 2.9 years) and higher parity (averaging 6.5 live births for women over age 45). The Casiguran Agta women similarly show a high total fertility (averaging 6.3 live births for women over 45) (Headland 1986:363). It is difficult to extrapolate from this fertility data the nature of past Agta populations, and it is, therefore, difficult to say whether these groups experienced higher, lower or the same level of fertility in the past.

Studies of the reproductive biology of hunter-gatherer populations indicate that they may have been subjected to a number of noncultural mechanisms of fertility control, which may have kept the fertility level low. Those mechanisms that may have affected fecundity of the Agta women in the past are their relative lack of body fat and the practice of prolonged breast-feeding.

The diet of hunter-gatherers tends to supply needed nutrients before the level of needed calories is reached (see Speth n.d.c), which results frequently in well-nourished but slender people (Howell 1980:192). Their high protein/low carbohydrate diet is also less congenial for accumulation of body fat (see Maynard and Loosli 1969). Frisch's (1974) "critical fatness hypothesis" suggests that low weight and slenderness among women can either prevent or delay pregnancies. Thus, Howell argues that the low fertility achieved among hunter-gatherers is perhaps due to the failure of women to maintain a critical fat level. Most Agta women, who weigh an average of 85 pounds (see Appendix 8; see also Headland 1986:544; Goodman et al. 1985:49), are slender. One can assume that the Agta women in the past, who probably had a higher protein diet as they had lower access to cultivated crops, were even more slender. If the critical fatness hypothesis is true, this is one Agta mechanism that may have played a role in their fertility control.

There is also the suggestion that prolonged breast-feeding delays pregnancy and thus results in low fertility. Lactation is believed to suppress or delay the return of ovulation during the postpartum period (Nag 1980:573). It thus can lengthen the average birth interval greatly among women of hunting and gathering societies, who breastfeed at high intensity over long periods of time (Howell 1980:191). The Agta women today tend to breastfeed their children for two to three years (see Estioko-Griffin 1985:29), and often wean them only a few months prior to the birth of the next born. There is no evidence to suggest that they did not do so in the past. If prolonged lactation does indeed inhibit conception, this may have been an important physiological mechanism for population control among the Agta. These physiological factors, individually or combined, may have kept the Agta fertility at a rate which was lower than today.

The mortality rate among the Agta in the past was also perhaps determined by only a few factors. While it has not been fully ascertained, the Agta groups did not seem to have practiced infanticide. Most Agta groups were not affected by the headhunting or the slave raiding practices of the non-Agta groups (Griffin 1985a:98). Suicide is rare today, as should have been the case in the past. Agta suffer only a few natural hazards such as typhoons, which generally do not cause deaths. There are few animals in these island forests that prey upon humans. While several individuals claim to have been attacked or bitten by large pythons, death from a python attack is rare. Sharks pose a threat during fishing in the open sea and crocodiles in rivers but the incidents are few. There are no reliable reports of Agta deaths from poisonous centipedes or snakes. Other accidents such as falling from a rock or tree during foraging trips occur but only infrequently. In fact, the only documented causes of violent death of the Agta in the past were due to the interlinguistic raiding, Agta-outsider vengeance killing and, among women, birth complications (see Headland 1986:390–92). Thus, the overall fatality rate among the Agta must have remained low in the past.

The Agta of northeastern Luzon do not seem to have suffered from major epidemic diseases in the remote past. This may have been due to the fact that these nomadic hunter-gatherers, living at a relatively low population density, were rarely exposed to epidemic diseases (Dunn 1968:23). However, following contact with outsiders, many hunter-gatherers have suffered from epidemic diseases. Among the Philippine groups, the Batak (see Warren 1964:5–6) and the Zambales Negritos (Blair and Robertson 1903–09, vol. 42:234; Garvan 1963:28) also occasionally suffered from localized smallpox and cholera epidemics.

A complex rain forest ecosystem such as that of the Agta contains diverse species of parasitic and infectious organisms with an equally diverse number of potential vectors as well as intermediate and alternate hosts (Dunn 1968:226). However, the local epidemiological history suggests that Agta themselves suffered from only a few diseases. Malaria was probably not prevalent as the Agta lived away from open agricultural fields (e.g., Harrison et al. 1977:233). Tuberculosis similarly remained unknown until recent times. The present population structure indicates that Agta do not suffer from sex-biased morbidity factors; the census of the Isabela Agta shows that the sex ratio remains equal across local and regional populations. It thus seems that the Agta suffered only from certain gastro-intestinal, pulmonary and a few other contagious diseases (see Headland 1986:394). These diseases were responsible for more deaths among children than adults.

In summary, the demographic conditions of the Agta in the past were characterized by both low fertility and mortality rates compared to their agricultural neighbors. If these conditions can be assumed, the Agta population trend was either fairly stable or rising only slowly. This population trend thus could not have produced population levels capable of creating sufficient pressure to initiate change. In short, changes in internal demographic conditions were perhaps relatively small, and population pressure was probably not a factor in bringing about Agta change.[1]

Population pressure is often calculated as a ratio of person-to-land. Such a ratio must, however, take into consideration the degree of availability of the resources used by the human groups; that is, a high population density itself is not an indicator of population pressure. While modern hunter-gatherers occupy a per capita land area of anywhere from 200 to 250 km^2 (Lee et al. 1968:11), there still are areas which, despite high population densities, have abundant resources (e.g., Shuttles 1968:56). Thus, to determine whether or not a group is actually experiencing population pressure, we need a better understanding of the person-to-resource ratio.

One such index popularly used in the anthropological studies is the *carrying capacity* of the ecosystem. In this index, a group is said to be experiencing population pressure when its given environment is over-exploited and thus adversely affected. However, the precise quantification of the carrying capacity of a particular ecosystem is a methodological nightmare (Odum 1975:12; Brush 1975). For example, for a human society, it is not the availability of resources, but their availability in culturally determined proportions that should dictate the level of carrying capacity of an area (Jochim 1976). A group exploits a given area only when a nexus of resources is available; absence or scarcity of one single important resource can limit its overall utilization. The nature of the settlement pattern of the group can affect the maximum sustainability of the area. The level of technology and the pattern of labor mobilization of the given group determine the carrying capacity. Finally, the determination of a culturally sensitive carrying capacity involves taking into consideration some of the unquantifiable variables; it is not only the availability of resources, but also the level of availability that is *perceived* as adequate by its occupants, that may determine the actual level of carrying capacity of the ecosystem.

All available evidence indicates that the Agta in the past maintained a high person-to-resource ratio, living well below the culturally determined carrying capacity of their environment and did not experience resource stress. They do not experience marked fluctuations in the availability of their traditional resources. Moreover, they have traditionally depended on a broad-spectrum subsistence strategy of hunting, gathering and fishing, so they have access to required quantities of wild food resources at any given time of the year. Time allocation studies show that the groups can extract a higher amount of such resources when the need arises (see Appendices 5 and 6; see also Headland 1986:313, 470).

Given that the Agta depend on a variety of wild starch resources, such as wild yam, caryota palm pulp, wild banana and other starchy fruits, they could have derived a sufficient amount of plant foods to meet their carbohydrate requirement. In the past, when the Agta ecosystem was much less degraded, they should not have experienced any scarcity of plant resources. A contrary view has, however, been advanced by Headland (1987b), who argues that the wild yam was not available in sufficient quantities in the northeastern Luzon rain forest in the past and therefore, the Agta could not have survived without some type of direct or indirect access to cultivated plant food resources. This argument is based on a number of assumptions and lacks substantive evidence regarding the importance of wild yam in the Agta diet in the past as well as the degree of unavailability of wild yam in the Agta forest. From my observation, wild yam is only one of the important plant foods, and it is exploited intensively for only a part of the year. One starchy fruit, *Diplodicus paniculatus*, was perhaps an even more important plant food for certain groups of Agta (Estioko-Griffin 1984:174). Other ethnobotanical studies hint that wild yam may have been more abundant in the past (Allen 1985:63), prior to environmental degradation.

For the Agta who depend heavily on hunting in their wild resource exploitation, the human-to-animal ratio is more relevant than the ratio of humans to plants. With the exception of large pythons (and crocodiles and sharks in specific locations), the Agta do not have to compete with other animal predators (Rai 1985:40). In the Agta rain forest there is also little niche competition among animals themselves. For example, the two large game animals on which the Agta primarily depend have different sources of food. The wild pig is an omnivorous animal but prefers food low in cellulose (nuts, fruits, tubers). Deer, on the other hand, are browsers and have diets which consist mainly of cellulose (grasses and leaves). Deer tend to feed in areas other than those preferred by the pigs. Agta claim that a thick undergrowth with large tall trees is frequented by deer whereas pigs are more abundant in forest areas having sparse undergrowth (Estioko and Griffin 1975:241).

The absence of interspecies predation and competition should mean abundance of these few game species. This is the case in particular Agta areas in Isabela today, and seems to have been the case in all Agta areas in the past. Spanish reports from other areas of the Philippines indicate an abundance of wild pig, deer and feral carabao (Blair and Robertson 1903–09, vol. 6:205, 21:197, 47:294–95). In addition to the oral histories, travellers in the Agta area in this century also attest to the abundance of wild pig and deer (Goddard 1930:330). These game animals provide the Agta with a major part of their subsistence today and should similarly have provided for them in the past. Moreover, besides the terrestrial game animals, the Agta had access to relatively rich aquatic faunal resources in the past to offset short-term food scarcities. They thus should have maintained a sustaining relationship with their environment without exerting stress on it. The historical records make no mention of the Agta ever experiencing famine or starvation (for similar data see Dunn 1968:223; Endicott 1979a:187).

A number of Agta cultural elements must have allowed the ecosystem to replenish, if they did not directly contribute to higher productivity. While Agta today do not exploit certain resource areas due to their belief that it would anger the supernatural spirits (see Rai 1985), they observe no taboos either in relation to wild food species or to particular times of the year; all the culturally known resources can be continuously exploited. Furthermore, the high mobility of the Agta results in reduced stress on resource locales and on individual food species, and thus, favors regeneration and growth of the food species.

The preceding analysis of the person-to-resource ratio supports the view that the Agta did not experience resource stress. This is also supported by the fact that in areas that have not been affected by outside encroachment, Agta continue to find traditional resources plentiful; informants claim that one can subsist on these traditional resources alone if one chooses to. Thus, in conclusion, it seems that the Agta experienced neither significant internal population growth nor the associated resource stress that could explain the change that they have undergone today.

External Conditions

In the absence of any substantial internal factors to account for the changes that have taken place among the Agta, we must seek the answer in the external system. The following is a description of external alterations and their role in bringing about change among the Agta.

There is circumstantial evidence to support the view that even in the remote past, the Agta did not live in total isolation from the adjoining agricultural and horticultural populations (see Griffin 1985a for a detailed review).

However, the Agta interaction with these populations was probably a peripheral and marginal one. The Agta seem to have continued to maintain their relative isolation throughout prehistoric and earlier historic times (Keesing 1962:361). The remoteness from highly populated agricultural areas and the rugged (and forested) terrain of their homeland inhibited large-scale immigration of outside agricultural people. Historical evidence indicates that whenever Agta were reached by outside populations, they escaped by retreating into the interior forest. Their foraging way of life, which was distinct from that of their neighbors, further contributed to their isolation from outsiders. The Agta remained little affected by the Spanish colonization of the Philippines. This isolation would end, however, as the adjoining lowland areas experienced major unheavals which would eventually come to disrupt the Agta traditional world in an unprecedented way.

The literature pertaining to Asian hunter-gatherers indicates that these technologically primitive people experienced intensive contact with outside agricultural and mercantile populations two centuries ago (e.g., Dahmen 1908; Hazewinkel 1935; Aiyappan 1948; Needham 1954; Watanabe 1968; Sinha 1972; Gardner 1972). These and other studies (e.g., Bennett 1969; Guenther 1976) strongly suggest that the contact of hunter-gatherers with outsiders initiated the early process of displacement of the hunter-gatherers.

There seem to be a number of reasons why hunter-gatherer areas are easily encroached upon. Hunter-gatherers are usually slow to react to outside incursion as they tend to believe that their resources are unlimited. The hunter-gatherers occupy large tracts of land relative to sedentary agricultural people. Today, the population density of non-Agta groups in Isabela is many times higher than that of the Agta; for example, the agricultural areas of San Mariano have a population density 72 times higher (see also Headland 1986:8). Consequently, there is a cultural misunderstanding among agricultural people who think that the hunter-gatherer area is underexploited and a *territorium nullis*—unoccupied and legally free for the taking (Bodley 1975:63). In their encroachment of the hunter-gatherer area, the agricultural population, therefore, does not realize that they are displacing the hunter-gatherers. While the universality of the above cases can be debated, the history of contact and encroachment on the Agta certainly followed the above scenario.

At first, only a few non-Agta swiddening populations formed the external population of the Agta groups. Since the beginning of this century the Agta experienced increasing contact with other immigrant agricultural populations who were in many ways different from the earlier indigenous horticultural populations.[2] These new immigrants brought a different land and resource use strategy which contrasted sharply with the traditional Agta foraging strategy. Because these non-Agta populations, indigenous and immigrant, had their own distinct languages and cultures, the ethnic mosaic became more complex. Pluralism rather than assimilation has become the norm, and these groups maintain social distance from one another as much as possible. Due to historical and other reasons, which will be described shortly, these different non-Agta groups vary markedly in their interaction with the Agta. The Agta themselves perceive this distinction among the non-Agta populations and distinguish between them accordingly.

The human taxonomy of the Agta has both generic and specific levels (see also Schebesta 1952/57:99). Generically, Agta distinguish humans (*tolay*) on the basis of the phenotypic features. All black people such as Agta, other Negrito people and American blacks, are classified under the taxon *agta*, and all non-black people under *tolay* (used at a more specific level of meaning). The *tolay* genus is further divided into three subgroups. The first, called *ogdin* among the Disabungan Agta, are the upland swiddeners who historically had inhabited areas adjoining the Agta. Today, this term is used to include the non-Christian indigenous minority groups. The second group, called *pote* by the Disabungan Agta (*pute* among other Agta linguistic groups; literally meaning "white") is the adjoining Christian populations who have been permanent settlers in the area for at least some decades. The third group, *tolay* (used at its most specific level of meaning), includes groups of outsiders who are temporary residents of the area (e.g., logging personnel, communist guerillas) and connotatively, those who do not speak the local trade language. For the sake of brevity, I have used the term "outsiders" here to include all the non-Agta populations of Isabela. I will specify their distinctions only when they are pertinent for the discussion.

On the valley watershed of the Sierra Madre in the province of Isabela, the areas immediately outside the Agta homeland are occupied by a horticultural group, locally called *kalinga*[3] (*ogdin* to the Agta). These Kalinga are a small population of subsistence swiddeners who have long inhabited a few frontier municipalities of Isabela. In the past, they used to practice what Conklin calls the "integral system" of shifting cultivation (1957:3). They cleared gardens in areas of pre-climax vegetation and maintained a swidden cycle of a one-year planting and fairly long fallow phase. Their established horticultural practices provided a viable subsistence at their relatively low population density. As they themselves were encroached upon by other agricultural groups, the Kalinga responded by encroaching on the Agta forest area. Today, as the encroachment and displacement continue, the Kalinga are socio-economically as distressed as the Agta and are retreating into the interior, following on the heels of the Agta. Forgetting that the Kalinga are indigenous swiddeners of the area, they are considered by the government to be illegal forest squatters (T: *kaingero*). The lack of political power and an ignorance of legal knowledge of land tenure among the Kalinga have contributed to their systematic dislocation by the immigrant, permanent field agricultural populations.

The Kalinga and Agta interacted rather closely in the past. Occasionally, inter-ethnic raids and killing occurred between the Agta and Kalinga. After such a confrontation, the elders came together to feast on a specially prepared rice cake cooked in pig fat (K: *kinalikob*) and settled their animosities. Informants from both groups agree that in the past the Disabungan Agta traded regularly with the Kalinga, although the latter also hunted to meet their protein needs. Today, while Agta trade with the Kalinga only minimally, they maintain other sociocultural exchanges. While intermarriages are still rare, social visits are very frequent. Agta frequently consult Kalinga shamanistic healers. Kalinga families are seen camping for short periods with Agta bands. Occasionally, they form collective hunting parties. In spite of the fact that there is no overt alliance, the Agta and Kalinga try to maintain amiable relations in the face of outside threat which is mutually felt by both groups.

Below the upland home of the Kalinga, the valley floor was originally inhabited by a number of Christian minority groups such as the Ibanag, Itawi, and Yogad (see Castillet 1960). These groups came under Spanish colonization in the nineteenth century, and after they were Christianized, they became loyal tenants of the local Spanish tobacco companies. Later, following the exploitation by these local tobacco companies, many of these minority groups fled the lowlands. At the same time, the large-scale outside immigration that was taking place in the Cagayan Valley also started displacing these minority groups from their floodplain homeland. Consequently, they were forced to take refuge in the upland areas and to displace both the horticultural Kalinga and the hunting and gathering Agta. While they were traditionally permanent field agriculturalists, they became part-time swiddeners in the upland areas.

These Christian minority groups differ linguistically from one another and they maintain social distance among themselves and from the Agta, the horticultural non-Christian groups and the immigrant Christian populations. According to informants, the Agta traded only occasionally in the past with these minority groups for cereals, tobacco and salt. Today, however, the Disabungan Agta bands trade more regularly with these groups.

By the end of the last century, the Ilokano immigrants outnumbered the local agricultural populations in particular valley bottom areas of the Cagayan Valley (McLennan 1980:112). Their rather aggressive economic strategies and sophisticated technologies for wet rice cultivation helped them to occupy the alluvial river terraces of the valley (Lewis 1971). By the 1920s, the alluvial areas of the Cagayan Valley were becoming saturated. Thus, as more Ilokano immigration continued, the later immigrants were forced to settle in the less favorable terrain of the uplands. Some groups immigrated directly into the frontier areas and encroached on the areas of the Agta. As the upland areas have fewer river terraces for permanent agriculture, the Ilokano immigrants became in part what Conklin calls "incipient swiddeners" (1957:3); they practiced swiddening without any prior knowledge of shifting cultivation.

The Agta of northeastern Luzon in general, and the Disabungan Agta in particular, maintain only a peripheral contact with the Ilokano. In spite of living adjacent to each other for at least three decades, Agta-Ilokano trade is irregular and cultural misunderstandings pervasive. While the Ilokano are known for their thriftiness, the egalitarian Agta see them as stingy (*médémmot*). They remain suspicious of Ilokano industriousness and see it as part of the intention to aggressively homestead the Agta forest area. The Ilokano informants similarly find the leisurely life of the Agta without motivation and incentive. They try to avoid extending any credit to the Agta because they find the Agta forgetfulness of commitments unforgivable.

All throughout history, the Agta have also been forced to interact with military organizations: antigovernment rebels and government forces that come to fight with the rebels. This group has included such diverse people as the Huk rebels, Japanese and American soldiers, the New People's Army and the Philippine military. While the Agta cannot comprehend why these people come when they come, and why they leave when they leave, they interact with them as trade partners and guides.

This outside population put pressure on the Agta population and their forest homeland. The first wave of pressure, from the beginning of the century to the 1920s, necessitated a number of adjustments in the Agta traditional world. These impacts were, however, relatively minor in comparison to what was to come in the following decades. With the beginning of large-scale mercantile activities during the American period of the Philippine history, and its intensification during the years immediately following the Philippines' independence (1950s), the Agta forest homeland came under intense mercantile pressure. The encroachment and exploitation of the Agta forest by the large-scale logging and mining activities were also radically different from the earlier agricultural encroachment. For example, while the earlier agricultural expansion was areally restricted and affected mostly low-lying river terraces, the mercantile activities concentrated on the high-canopy interior forest. While the Agta could escape the earlier agricultural expansion by retreating into the interior areas, the mercantile activities in the heart of the Agta forest home engulfed them.

For a number of reasons, the Agta themselves underestimate the impact of logging and mining activities in their forest home and do not seem to really resent this form of encroachment. For example, the logging and mining companies are interested in resources (e.g., dipterocarp trees, mineral ores) with which the Agta themselves are not directly concerned; the Agta do not see themselves in direct resource competition with the mercantile population. In addition, this population has become the new trade partners for the Agta and mercantile stations, the new trade nuclei. They also provide sporadic employment for the Agta as well as shuttle transportation to and from agricultural settlements or nearby towns.

Agta are, however, well aware of one of the effects of these mercantile activities in their area; these activities lead to further increased immigration of outside populations. The mercantile companies with their need for skilled workers, available only from outside, have encouraged the immigration process. A 1979 survey of San Mariano Municipality shows that of the 4,210 families permanently residing in the municipality, 39 percent of the families claimed to have come recently to this area from outside the municipality and approximately half of these immigrant families from outside the province of Isabela (MDS 1979:6,12). New immigrants brought in with the mercantile companies have come to establish many frontier settlements, including a few towns.

The mercantile population remains seasonally idle as the logging and mining operations stop during the peak northeast monsoon. Taking advantage of the free use of heavy logging and mining machinery from the companies, this mercantile population claims vast forest areas for garden clearing and homesteading. They recruit their kin to immigrate to these frontiers. Perhaps as a natural response to living for generations in densely populated areas, to these new immigrants the "empty" forest lands seem endless and they invite their kin to homestead with them on the new frontiers.

In recent years, the largest wave of immigration to the Sierra Madre is composed of populations from the Central Cordillera, which lies immediately to the west of the Cagayan Valley. Groups such as the Ifugao and Tinguian, who are well known for their intricate rice-terracing, had lived in the congested mountain areas for centuries. Following serious land and population pressures, these groups have become willing immigrants in these frontiers in search of a new home. These groups show an interesting pattern in their encroachment on the Agta forest. Unlike the earlier immigrants, who encroached on the forest land from its fringes, these recent immigrants have pioneered directly into the middle of the forest, colonized the forest valleys and expanded from there. By taking over the arable land even in the remote Agta areas, these homesteaders have created colonies of agricultural people in the center of the Agta homeland.

The Central Cordillera people immigrate in relatively large groups. Once settled, the communities protect themselves against other outside incursion and maintain a marked socioeconomic isolation from their neighbors; these are the cultural practices of the groups in their places of origin. While in the early years of their immigration, they faced a number of economic hardships, today they have become economically successful. The more established groups practice dry field and irrigated rice cultivation through terracing. Because of their economic success, many more people who were originally reluctant are also immigrating into the area. The Agta, who call these immigrants *Igorot*, intensely fear their alleged powers of witchcraft and sorcery, and contact between the Agta and Igorot has always been minimal.

In summary, while the Agta were experiencing only small changes in their traditional system, the external, agricultural and mercantile encroachment acted as a catalyst to bring about a number of changes to the Agta environment. The net immigration of the outside population raised the population density of the area many-fold. The chain of events of immigration, encroachment, land expansion and colonization affected the original ratio of the Agta to their land and resources. As it will be made clear later, the outside population temporarily raised the carrying capacity of the Agta environment by providing new economic avenues and technologies to exploit the previously unused resources. However, these new economic enterprises themselves brought further alterations as they required the Agta to move away from a traditional world toward a transitional world.

9
The Economic Transition

The changing conditions of the Agta traditional world have brought about transformations in both natural and sociocultural realms. Of these, the traditional economy of the Agta is most visibly affected and thus, the economic transition is perhaps pre-eminent. To begin with, following the external encroachment, the Agta forest home is shrinking and their physical resources are becoming depleted. As if to compensate for this loss, Agta have become economically interdependent with, and often dependent on, external populations through the practice of economic exchange. Historical evidence from northeastern Luzon strongly supports the view that the Agta interdependence with the outside population intensified only in the last two centuries (e.g., Garvan 1963). Because such an intensified interdependence is the culmination of both local historical and economic processes, we must not only ask when the interaction between the Agta and the outside population began, but also why such an interdependency became necessary. This chapter will analyze the Agta economic transition by juxtaposing the probable local historical sequences with the local as well as regional economic situations. Any subsistence strategy which was not part of the traditional Agta economy but which was developed in conjunction with the outside population will be called a nonforaging strategy. In the Agta economic transition, there are three such subsistence strategies. Following their general order of economic importance to the Agta today, they are: trade, horticulture and wage labor.

Trade

The egalitarian Agta families (or bands) do not carry out direct economic exchange with their counterparts; among Agta, traditional economic goods move only through the social mechanism of sharing. The term *trade* or *exchange* is thus used here to denote the inter-ethnic economic transactions of the Agta with the non-Agta populations and which involves the exchange of forest, riverine and marine products for nontraditional items. Today, trading has become the most important subsistence strategy of the Agta. The items exchanged include both food and non-food items. The Agta trade both with the adjoining but economically dissimilar agricultural groups and with groups with primarily mercantile practices.

Barter trade in forest products is an old practice among the hunter-gatherers of Asia (Dunn 1975:00; Morris 1977:228), though the products varied across regions of Asia and across the centuries. The trade among hunter-gatherers in the Philippines has similar antiquity. Since at least the twelfth century, the coastal populations began trading with hunter-gatherers (and horticulturalists) inhabiting the uplands and interior portion of the island (Hutterer 1977:192).

Assuming that Hutterer's (1977) general model of the upland-coastal exchange holds true for northeastern Luzon, where the Agta were the predominant uplanders (Keesing 1962), we can surmise that the Agta had begun trading with coastal dwellers in pre-Hispanic times. On the assumption that the Agta always needed a supply of domestic carbohydrate, Headland (1987b) suggests that the Agta were practicing *intense* trade with their non-Agta neighbors as long ago as 2000 B.C. While we lack clear evidence to claim such long antiquity of Agta trade, we can assume that they were trading for salt (only a few Agta groups today know how to extract salt from sea water) as well as possibly metal during the pre-Hispanic time (possibly since the twelfth century). By Spanish times, some Philippine Negrito groups were bartering beeswax (which was used to stiffen thread for the Hispanic looms) for tobacco (Rahmann 1963:144). The Spanish record directly pertaining to the Agta of northeastern Luzon (see Headland 1986:194–217 for a detailed review) speaks of the Agta groups having erratic economic relations with their neighbors; at times, particular groups of Agta were trading, while at other times, this economic exchange was halted because the agricultural and horticultural populations were said to fear the Agta. The historical evidence allows us to assume rather confidently that while some trade relations between the various Agta groups and their horticultural and agricultural neighbors did exist in the sixteenth century, it was probably carried out only intermittently by specific groups for specific trade goods (see Griffin 1985a:87). The Agta may not have traded meat of wild game, as the agricultural and horticultural populations procured it themselves by hunting.

Sometime between the seventeenth and nineteenth centuries, the horticultural and agricultural groups seem to have begun living in relatively closer proximity to the Agta (Keesing 1962:258). Following this, it seems that the list of barter items as well as the volume of the inter-ethnic trade expanded (see Semper 1861; Segovia 1969; Philippine Commission 1908). One of the items for which the Agta bartered their forest products was domestic cereals.

The Agta trade (*palit*) of wild products for domestic cereals has greatly increased today. In particular areas, the trade between Agta and their adjoining neighbors has become institutionalized in the sense that it is done predominantly through formal trade partnership. From the perspective of Agta groups who have entered it, the trade partnership (*ibay*; also *ahibay*, *aribay*, or *alibay*) is a very important one. It demands a commitment to regular exchange, and allows extension of credit, and it commits the partners to other economic transactions as needed (Peterson 1978a:80). This formal trade partnership is established between a married Agta adult (male or female) and a married male from the neighboring agricultural group (Estioko-Griffin et al. 1981:134).

A number of researchers have documented the institution of trade partnership (e.g., Peterson 1978a, 1978b; Headland 1986). However, it should be pointed out that these descriptions are meant for specific groups of Agta, such as from Palanan and Casiguran, and they hold true only for these groups. In other words, the institution of trade partnerships is not universal among all Agta groups. The evidence that this partnership is a localized phenomenon comes from the fact that it has been reported only from particular coastal areas of northeastern Luzon. In other areas of the coastal watershed and in many areas of the valley watershed, this institution is not formally recognized by the Agta themselves or by their agricultural counterparts; in these places there are neither regular trade partnerships nor commitments to long-term economic transactions between trading individiuals.

In all probability, the localized, inter-ethnic trade partnership was also a phenomenon of relatively recent development. Traditionally, there were a number of factors that hindered any long-term trade partnership between an Agta individual and an outsider. For example, the small, neighboring agricultural populations may have met most of their needs for forest products by themselves. Because Agta intensely distrust outsiders, and this feeling is reciprocated, such mutual suspicion may well have caused the break-up of trade relationships. Additionally, frequent mobility of the Agta must have been responsible for severing some economic transactions with the settled outsiders. The formalized trade partnerships that exist today are only among Agta groups who have become semi-sedentary, and are probably only as old as the beginning of this century at most.

Economic exchange through formal trade partnership is only part of the total Agta trade. This is because even among Agta groups who establish a formal partnership, the relationship is rarely a permanent and stable one. In many cases, the agreement is not well understood by the parties involved. There is no recognizable social event (e.g., gift giving) to initiate the trade partnership and there is uncertainty concerning its termination. Agta informants seem often in doubt as to whether or not a particular trade partnership is current. Moreover, these Agta groups must trade a good volume in commercial goods with individual dealers and contractors who do not maintain an ongoing, formal trading partnership. As we will see shortly, Agta sell tree resin, seashells, and other goods to professional buyers who usually come from outside the trade settlements and this trade of commercial items, in fact, provides for the bulk of Agta exchange needs (see Headland 1986:326).

The overall trade relationship between the Agta and outsiders, with or without the formal trade partnership, has been considerably modified in recent decades. While in the last century, Agta were engaged in barter trade of a few forest products against an equally small number of outside commodities (salt, tobacco, cereals, etc.), the monetized trade of today has come to include a myriad of other wild products and numerous consumer goods.

Today, the most regular, and for most groups, the largest by volume, trade item of the Agta of Isabela is animal protein, both terrestrial and aquatic. The Agta of the valley watershed trade a higher volume of terrestrial animal protein than those of the coastal watershed who also trade aquatic protein. The neighboring agricultural populations, of the respective watersheds attest to this pattern when they stereotype those Agta of the valley watershed as primarily hunters and those of the coastal watershed as fishing people. The items traded, however, do not include all the various game animals and aquatic fauna that are exploited by the Agta. Only the meat of wild pig and deer is traded and usually only eel, octopus, and lobster, and the bigger varieties of fish are exchanged.

The Agta claim that animal protein is their primary trade item for two reasons. First, with an increased outsider population in the area today, there is a ready and always reliable market for it as opposed to other forest products. The adjoining agricultural populations raise a few domestic animals, and they occasionally hunt, but this does not regularly meet the growing need for animal protein.[1] In addition to the demands of the large agricultural population, wild game and fish are also in demand by the mercantile populations. Second, animal protein is the Agta wild product which has the highest market value. Agta clearly see these advantages and depend on the trade of animal protein for these reasons.

Calorically, the trade of animal protein for cereals means a high energy return in exchange. For example, in 1980, 1 kg of meat was worth 10 pesos, or 5 kg of rice or 10 kg of corn. Thus, when 1 kg of meat (3,070 Cal/pig or 920 Cal/deer) was exchanged for cereals (18,100 Cal/rice or 38,600 Cal/corn; see Appendix 9), the caloric return in exchange was in a ratio of 1:6 (pig:rice) and 1:41 (deer:corn). The trade of animal protein is thus energetically efficient when compared to other subsistence strategies. For example, Agta take less than three adult hours to acquire 1 kg of meat, which when traded returns 18,100 Cal of rice or 38,600 Cal of corn. If Agta were to choose to dig the most common wild root in its most abundant season for the same three hours, they would procure approximately 3 kg of wild root (2,900 Cal). The return from digging wild roots would be six times lower than the trade of meat for rice or fourteen times lower than the trade for corn.

The volume and frequency of the Agta trade of animal protein is determined primarily by the degree of their deficit of domestic carbohydrate, for which they have developed a taste for and dependence on. Peterson (1977b), however, suggests that the regular Agta trade of animal protein is also due to their protein surfeit. Peterson writes that " ... even a single boar ... represents a protein surfeit for a camp group, and the usual kill exceeds this amount" (1977b:69). My data indicate that such a surfeit of animal protein is not likely to occur among the Agta, due to the calculated rate of game procurement and the practice of sharing among and between bands. The data from the Disabungan River, which is still one of the most productive hunting areas for the Isabela Agta, and which is represented by the bands who hunt most frequently, substantiate the argument that Agta do not experience protein surfeit. In a total of 64 days' observation across a three-month period, one band of the Disabungan Agta (21 people) were acquiring one large game animal (pig or deer) every two days (see Appendix 7). The animals weighed on an average of 22 kilograms.[2] When the meat was shared (and eaten over a two-day period), each individual should have eaten a maximum of .5 kg/day.[3] My observations of Agta meat consumption were that adults can and do consume one kilogram in a single day. Thus, from the point of view of the Agta, there is no protein surfeit. One may argue that the procurement of game animals is not evenly spaced across days and months and that it might bring erratic surfeits. During the northeast monsoon season, hunting is better (and the trade is minimal), but the Disabungan Agta did not claim to experience any surfeit of animal protein even at this peak season. A combination of hunting and fishing could conceivably result in an animal protein surfeit, but in any given day, only one strategy is usually applied to meet the food requirement. Fishing in the lucrative coastal areas could possibly bring an occasional surfeit but it is also seriously limited by the existing technology.

Another line of evidence that the Agta trade of animal protein is not determined by the surfeit is that today the percentage of meat of wild animals to be traded is culturally predetermined. Agta never sell the whole game animal (pig or deer) no matter how many are killed on a particular day. When trade is to be done, Agta scrupulously set aside particular parts of game (which vary by linguistic groups) for trade. Among the Disabungan Agta, only the hindquarters (*pukél*), the forequarters (*sahap*) and the lower portion of the back (*sépang*) are traded in the case of wild pig. In the case of deer, in addition to the above parts, the head (*buntok*) and the neck (*léyas*) are also traded. Any trade of excessive meat outside the culturally predetermined parts is proscribed by the norm of Agta sharing.

The difference between pig and deer meat-trading practices is related to the food preferences of the two populations involved in trade. While Agta universally find the taste of wild pig savory, the agricultural and mercantile people in general consider deer a delicacy and prefer it over wild pig. Due to this preference and consequently due to the trade of predetermined parts, the percentage of a particular kind of game traded varies. The Disabungan Agta were trading on the average only 42% of the wild pig as opposed to 75% of deer. By gross weight of the two primary kinds of game animals, the Agta band was trading on an average day 6.2 kg of meat (3.4 kg of pig and 2.8 kg of deer) and consuming 5.6 kg of meat (4.7 kg of pig and 0.9 kg of deer) (see Appendix 7). Of course, the traded parts consisted of better meat and the consumed parts comprised bone and internal organs which were considered less desirable by the Agta themselves.

Evidence that the Agta trade of animal protein stems from a growing dependence on and deficit of domestic cereals, and not from a surfeit of animal protein, comes from a number of observations. Agta do little trading of animal protein when they are intensively digging wild yams or when they are harvesting their own swidden crops. Agta frequently borrow cereals to be paid for later in meat or fish and thus there is always an outstanding trade deficit. Agta actually consume far less in amount (on an average, .25 kg primary game meat per person per day) than they would want to. Thus, Agta are regularly sacrificing more desirable animal protein so that they can offset the deficit of domestic cereals.

Among coastal Agta groups, on which Peterson's argument for protein surfeit was based, hunting is emphasized less than it is among the interior groups. Also, among these coastal groups, the exchange value of animal protein, including fish, is about half of what it is in the valley watershed. In these areas, the Agta must trade larger volumes of the animal protein to meet the same degree of demand in domestic carbohydrates. This was probably the case in the past as well; while the Agta were less dependent on outside carbohydrates, they then received even a lower exchange rate for their animal protein. For example, in the Disabungan area, the exchange rate in the 1960s was approximately eight times lower than in the late 1970s. Agta had to trade more frequently and in larger meat volume to meet what was then a relatively small demand of domestic carbohydrate.

A particular tree resin, popularly known as Manila copal (*saléng, Agathis philippinesis*), is one of the important nonfaunal forest product of the Agta. Among particular groups of Asian hunter-gatherers, the trading of tree resin was practiced prehistorically (e.g., Morris 1977:235) and today it has become an important source of livelihood (e.g., Eder 1978). The available oral history of the northeastern Luzon also suggests that the trade of copal resin has been going on at least since the early decades of this century and for particular Agta linguistic groups, it has become an important trade activity today. According to informants, this tree resin can be collected year round. To tap the resin, the tree bark is cut and the sap allowed to bleed out. The resin is left to dry for one to three months. One person can collect one sack (approximately 40 kg) of dried resin per day, which had a market value of

40 pesos in Isabela in 1979. It is sold to dealers specifically designated by the government as registered contractors.

In varying degree, the Agta groups also collect and trade varieties of rattan and bamboo. Some Agta groups (viz., Dikaméy and Maconacon) occasionally barter mats and containers made from varieties of screw pines. They also occasionally trade honey, orchids, panicles of tiger grass (*boyboy*, *Phragmites vulgaris*) for broom-making and shingles of nipa palm (*sépsép*, *Nipa fruiticans*) as thatch material. In recent years, a particular group of coastal Agta (Palanan) has practiced commercial shell fishing. They collect two varieties of shellfish (*samong* and *lérang*), eat the meat and trade the shells. Agta also occasionally collect medicinal herbs at the request of outsiders. Most of the secondary trade items of the Agta are collected and traded to acquire domestic cereals, other consumer goods such as liquor, and often for payment of debt incurred in earlier exchanges.

Trade is the most important transitional economic strategy of the Agta and is used primarily as a means to import outside cereals and other consumer goods. Today, particular groups of Agta may go for days without a substantial intake of foraged food, such as meat and fish, but there are comparatively few days without the consumption of the traded food (see Headland 1986:459). In the overall ranking of the Agta food items today, cereals (particularly rice) may rank as high as wild animal meat, if not higher, and definitely higher than fish. Thus, today, the total caloric contribution of trade to the Agta diet is very high; Disabungan Agta derive 55% of their total caloric intake through the food items obtained in trade; 95% of their non-forest food diet is from trade food (see Appendix 10). During one observation period, the Disabungan Agta males were devoting 15% of their working time to trade-related activities and females were devoting 33% of their working time to this activity (see Appendix 6). In terms of caloric expenditure, these males and females were spending 18% and 24%, respectively, of their total caloric output in trade-related activities (see Appendix 12).

The Agta trade of forest products for outside foods and consumer goods has in turn brought a number of other economic transformations to their traditional system. It played a major role in leading the Agta to become dependent on the outside population. As we will see later, the nature and intensity of the Agta-outsider trade transactions determined in many ways the course of the present Agta transition.

Horticulture

The second important nonforaging subsistence strategy for most groups of the Isabela Agta is the practice of horticulture. While, on the one hand, the Philippine Negritos were stereotyped by missionaries and colonial administrators as "people without cultivation" even at the beginning of this century (e.g., Barrows 1908:45–46), Fox has suggested that the cultivation of certain indigenous plants must have been practiced by these groups for three to four thousand years (1953:247). On the basis of historical and ecological evidence, Brosius has argued that the Negritos of Zambales had become regular swiddeners during the Spanish time and possibly even prior to then (1981:94, 124). This evidence indicates that particular groups of the Philippine Negritos have been practicing some degree of horticulture since the pre-Hispanic times.

The specific history of horticulture practices among the Agta of northeastern Luzon is vague. Agta oral history lacks reference to any cultivation (Headland 1975b:294) or cultivated plants. While one can assume that some Agta groups were practicing some form of swiddening by the Spanish time (see Headland 1986), they took up horticulture on a more regular basis only as late as the beginning of this century (see Worcester 1912:841). As the Agta interaction with outsiders increased, their horticultural activity seems to have become extensive; all middle-aged informants from groups of the Isabela Agta claim that their parents were practicing swiddening during World War II. Given this description, horticulture is a more recent nonforaging strategy of the Agta compared to trade.

The swiddens (*sikaw*) of the Isabela Agta are usually located upriver along the river terraces and adjacent slopes. Depending upon the topography of the river valley and the size of Agta population in the area, the Agta gardens nucleate at a few locations, usually close to the more frequently used campsites. Such a clustering of gardens in specific parts of the river valley occurs because the closely related band members prefer to clear gardens in one area separate from the gardens of non-kin from other bands.

The horticultural calendar of the Agta roughly follows that of the adjoining horticultural and agricultural populations. If the families in a band decide to cultivate in a given year, the preparation for garden clearing begins immediately following the northeast monsoon. The Agta system of horticulture uses a long fallow cycle (Boserup 1965:15); as much as possible, they select a previously cleared area but one that has lain fallow for a number of years. Agta claim to prefer bush over secondary forest, and secondary forest over primary forest or Imperata grassland. In February or March, the first stage of garden clearing begins by cutting the underbrush and small trees with machetes; collective labor of adult males and occasionally females is used. In the second stage, adult males cut down the big trees with steel axes. Trees with canopies are always cut down, while palms, wild fruit trees and commercially valuable hardwoods may be saved. The clearing is left to dry for some months; since this area has a number of rainy days in any given month, burning would otherwise be difficult. The felled vegetation is set afire in April or May, and any remaining may be again gathered into piles and burnt.

A particular Agta garden may be planted with only a few crops at a time. However, as Agta practice intercropping, the list of cultivated plants in one Agta garden can be long. The most commonly planted crops are sweet potato, cassava, corn, upland rice, yam and taro. A number of vegetables such as squash, snake gourd, eggplant, garlic and ginger are also planted in small quantities. Occasionally Agta gardens have papaya, coconut, jackfruit, banana and sugar cane. Tobacco is said to do poorly in swiddens and thus is rarely planted.

Most Agta do not own draft animals. Sometimes they borrow them from an agricultural neighbor, but in general they do not use any animal energy in their gardening. Their "non-hoe cultivation" (Boserup 1965:23) is done with few tools. The swiddening families plant their crops with a wooden dibble stick (*ésad*). Agta borrow seeds from their agricultural neighbors to plant the "rainy season" crops during the months of June or July. Collective labor is usually summoned to plant upland rice, which is done in teams. The remaining adjacent clearings are planted with sweet potato and vegetables in May. Vegetables are picked throughout the year, and rice is harvested in October or November with a special sickle (*arakém*). This is followed by the harvest of sweet potato up until January. The area is partially cleared for the planting of "dry season" crops. The first planting of cassava and second planting of sweet potato are done in December or January. Corn is planted in April or May and harvested in the following July or August. Sweet potato is harvested from May to August and cassava from October to December to supplement the intervening periods. As Agta think that the gardens are less productive in the second year of cultivation, they move to an adjacent patch to clear gardens for the next horticultural year.

The Agta swiddening in general remains desultory. The Disabungan Agta families who practice horticulture claim an average of approximately one hectare of swidden land. In a given year, these families actually clear only about one-fourth of the total swidden area to plant their crops. As Agta gardens are isolated in patches surrounded by the primary forest, their swiddening is perhaps more susceptible to diseases and insects (see Olsen, Clark and Bennett 1981:380). Further, the gardening techniques of the Agta continue to remain haphazard. Because of the mobility and frequent absence from their respective gardens, Agta find it difficult to follow a horticultural calendar. Thus, the unsystematic clearing, burning and planting and the lack of weeding, fencing and guarding result in poor crop production. An observation showed that in the months of August and September (which are not peak horticultural months), a band of Disabungan Agta (who are probably the least horticulturally oriented) spent as little as one percent of their working time in tending their gardens (see Appendix 6). Another observation showed that a garden plot of a hectare produces approximately 1,000 kg of upland rice. This production is 38 percent lower than the average production of upland rice (1,600 kg/ha) of swiddens of the adjoining non-Agta population (PDA 1978:55).

There are other factors which keep the contribution of horticulture to the Agta diet low. For example, practice of horticulture by Agta families is not consistent; one year, they cultivate and the next few years, they may not. Perhaps typical of foragers-turned-horticulturalists, the Agta apply the foraging technique to harvesting crops; they usually harvest their crops in portions that are required for the day and tend to "eat" on one garden at a time and move to the next in succession. Due to this, destruction of harvest-ready crops by rain, wind and animals (particularly birds and insects) is high. Further, irrespective of whether or not they have contributed labor to clearing or planting the swidden, a number of other families may join the cultivator's band in harvesting the crop and sharing the produce. Because of the sharing of cultivated crops with families who may not own gardens, in a given year, the per capita caloric intake from Agta cultivation is low. During the month of October, the Disabungan Agta were deriving only approximately 4 percent of their total caloric intake from their horticulture (see Appendix 10). Of the nonforest food items, the products of horticulture formed 8 percent of the Agta caloric intake. My estimate is that even among the most horticulture-oriented bands of the Isabela Agta, the caloric contribution of their horticulture does not exceed 20 percent of their total caloric intake. Among the Casiguran Agta, who are among the most horticulture-oriented groups, their produce lasts for less than one and a half months (Headland 1986:349).

While horticulture plays only a subsidiary economic role, it has brought its own consequences. As we will see later, the Agta horticultural sites act as the entry points from where the outside population reclaims an area for homesteading.

Wage Labor

The third, and least important, nonforaging economic activity of the Isabela Agta today is wage labor.

The practice of laboring for wages (*upa*) is an interesting development among the Agta. Wage labor was not traditionally practiced by the Agta. They have no word for "helper" or "slave" and the word with the closest meaning one can translate is "friend" (*aghum*). Wage labor activity probably developed only after the Agta had intensified relationships with outsiders. It seems, therefore, that wage labor is a subsidiary Agta economic strategy, participated in by particular groups of the Agta since only relatively recent times.

The earliest reference to the Agta practice of wage labor comes from Semper (1861), who observed that in 1860s the Agta of San Mariano were working for the Irraya (probably Kalinga) neighbors. Early in this century, certain Agta groups from particular coastal areas also started hiring themselves out as porters (*cargador*) or guides to their neighbors. The coastal agricultural settlements around Palanan and Casiguran Bay had to depend on overland access to the Cagayan Valley. Agta living close to these settlements hauled both goods and people and acted as guides across the forested Sierra Madre ridge. Even today, particular groups continue to pursue portering. Agta load carriers, mostly males and occasionally females, transport mats, hats, or chickens out of the coastal towns and bring in an equal weight of outside commodities such as tobacco and cloth. It will be recalled that these coastal areas were also the only areas where the formal Agta-outsider trade partnership developed, and this institution continues today. Thus, it seems that the Agta practice of portering must have developed as they incurred indebtedness following the formal trade partnerships.

Today, most groups of Isabela Agta participate in the practice of agricultural wage labor. Among certain coastal groups who live close to the agricultural settlements, there are families who depend heavily on agricultural labor (see Headland 1986:329–30; W. Peterson 1981:48–49). Others engage in this activity only during the harvest season. As the harvest season approaches, Agta families camp close to the agricultural settlements and help harvest the crops. Judging from the volume of grain these Agta families bring back to the camp, they derive considerable income from this activity.

Occasionally, an Agta individual, or even a family, will provide resident labor to an agricultural household, a practice that has occurred since the last century (see Semper 1861, 1869; Worcester 1913:88). Orphans, particularly females, or families of widows leave their Agta bands to reside permanently in agricultural households to help in domestic and agricultural works (see Headland 1986:266).

More recently, Agta have been given sporadic employment at the local logging and mining companies. The mercantile population believes, erroneously, that an Agta band is ruled by a territorial leader who is apt to mobilize his band members to mount operations that can disrupt the mercantile activities in the area. Thus, in order to maintain good public relations, those they believe to be the leaders are hired to work as guides, scouts or guards. This form of employment pays a monthly wage and occasional gifts of liquor and cigarettes. Even more recently, the immigrant homesteaders have begun hiring Agta on a contract basis to clear forest for swidden or agricultural land.

Agta do not like the constraints imposed by the wage labor practice, which often require them to live alone away from their band members. It is also considered a menial job by the more traditional Agta. On the other hand, wage labor is becoming an economic opportunity Agta families can no longer ignore. For groups who intensively practice it, it has become an important subsistence strategy in their changing economics. In differing degrees, it has already brought change to all Agta groups. For families and bands involved in wage labor, it has constricted their practice of camp movement and consequently, exploitation of traditional resources. Thus, the practice of wage labor is encouraging the Agta to be totally dependent on the outsider population.

The Agta groups of Isabela today have incorporated three nonforaging economic strategies: trade, horticulture and wage labor. Due to different historical and demographic factors, the groups differ in their practice of these three strategies. In general, however, trade is the most important nonforaging activity followed by horticulture and wage labor in that order. These three strategies have either individually or in combination brought about an economic transition among the Agta. Concomitantly, the Agta have de-emphasized their reliance on the traditional economic strategies and resource bases. In most cases, the Agta groups have lost traditional economic self-sufficiency. Instead of being independent, they have become critically dependent on the outside agricultural populations, who, as will be shown later, could maintain an economic system independent of the Agta.

10
The Consequences

The external encroachment on the Agta forest homeland as well as the dependence of the Agta on the non-Agta population have resulted in a number of changes in the traditional Agta world. The consequences are particularly visible in the degradation of the Agta ecosystem, the associated economic readjustments and the economic and socio-symbolic subordination of the Agta by the outsiders.

Ecological Degradation

The stability of the natural communities of the Agta rain forest has been emphasized above. Until the recent centuries, the Agta foragers were the only people who exploited these forests and their impact on the ecosystem was minimal (e.g., Rambo 1979:63, 64). While the neighboring agricultural groups extracted particular game and certain forest products such as deer antler and beeswax, this exploitation was peripheral. These selective human interventions may have acted in a small way as modifiers of the inter-specific composition of the rain forest ecosystem (Grime 1979:41), bringing about small changes in it (Hutterer 1985:62). Otherwise, the human groups effected little change in the Agta rain forest ecosystem.

The large-scale exogenous intervention, particularly in this century, has, however, brought both qualitative and quantitative changes to the Agta ecosystem (e.g., Raven 1981:28). The greatest external force that directly exploits this primary forest is that of mercantile logging and mining operations.

The logging companies in Isabela follow selective tree-cutting techniques; they cut only larger trees of certain diameter. There are two views on the merits of such selective logging. One view is that the technique of selective logging only depletes the forest of certain species of trees but that it does not constitute a major disturbance of the forest system because the gap left by the exploited trees is quickly filled by similar tree species (Slatyer 1977:13). The other view is that areas of primary forest subjected to selective exploitation in fact do become depleted as the gaps left by the removal of timber are colonized by dissimilar, secondary forest species (Richards 1979:379).

Empirical studies in the Philippines support the view that large-scale selective logging brings a marked vegetative succession of secondary forest species. Brown and Mathews claim that direct sunlight exposure brought about by selective logging causes young trees with poorly developed crowns to die (1914:536). Selective logging also brings mechanical damage to the forest as the cutting of trees with large crowns breaks and kills a large proportion of smaller surrounding ones. In addition, trail construction for the logging operation creates disturbances all over the primary forest area.

The aftermath of the perturbation of the tropical rain forest like that found in the Agta area is obvious. The extensive perturbation of the original structure of the vegetative community initiates and enhances the succession of vegetation (Farnworth and Golley 1974:118). Forests are efficient water reservoirs in times of heavy rainfall. By retaining a large volume of water and releasing it gradually, they protect the area from floods and landslides. Removing this check increases the rate of environmental degradation. The primary forest plant community lives on meager soil nutrients, which are hoarded and maintained by the rapid recycling of dead organisms. This retrieval system is lost if the complex processes of weathering, leaching of nutrients and other biological activity (e.g., organic decomposition and nitrogen fixation) cannot take place (Colinvaux 1978:76; Olsen et al. 1981:378). These can bring about significant changes in the tropical forest vegetation, and when it is severe, the original natural system can be completely lost (Slayter 1977:6). This trend is clearly observed in the Agta rain forest, particularly since the terrain is highly inclined and subject to heavy monsoon precipitation, both of which further aggravate the problem.

If the impact of mercantile operations were not enough to seriously degrade the Agta ecosystem, the expansion of the agricultural populations effected this process. Given high immigration, the continuing encroachment by the agricultural population was inevitable. While today the low-lying valley bottoms support the majority of the agricultural population, the land and population pressures are mounting there. To escape these pressures, the agricultural population is encroaching upon the terraces further upriver and as the river terraces run out, the forest slopes. The forest area that has been logged-over by the mercantile companies is preferred because the big trees have been felled and removed from the area and relatively little initial labor investment is required to homestead and cultivate it. Understandably, the immigrants are eager to follow the mercantile operation and appropriate such logged-over areas.

Tropical uplands like the Agta area tend to be less amenable to permanent field agriculture. Agricultural activity usually involves maintaining low plant diversity. As the tropical ecosystem has a high species diversity, the practice of permanent agriculture calls for a large input in the form of mechanical and chemical work (Odum 1975:52). In the Sierra Madre, the clay loam volcanic soil is prone to soil erosion and lateralization. In the absence of terrace agriculture, proper technology and fertilizers, cultivated fields in these uplands quickly become unproductive. People who have the option of claiming land areas in the adjoining forest will abandon the old fields and encroach upon the forest. This cycle of cultivating the land for a few years and abandoning it in favor of new clearings in the forest results in the deforestation of the uplands.

The uplands in northeastern Luzon could sustain the practice of horticulture if an appropriate swiddening cycle was followed. However, in the Agta area, the rampant agricultural expansion by the nonswiddening population threatens the traditional, integral practices of swiddening by indigenous groups such as the Kalinga. Encircled by the agricultural groups with their permanent cultivated fields, the indigenous horticultural groups are under pressure not to follow the established cycle of shifting cultivation. They are attempting to change their swiddens into permanent dry fields bringing further ecological consequences to the area (see Wallace 1970b:75-76). Adding to this problem is the fact that those new immigrants who have become the incipient swiddeners do not know how to maintain a sustainable cycle in their practice of shifting cultivation (e.g., Conklin 1957:155). Thus, the land expansion of the outside population, be it for permanent agriculture or horticulture, is bringing devastating ecological consequences to the Agta forest area.

The tropical rain forest plant community is considered to be highly resilient in its natural state. However, when the disturbance is severe, its complete recovery is impossible (Colinvaux 1978:208; Dasmann et al. 1973:48, 58). Observation in the affected area of the Agta forest also indicates that it does not recover from such disturbances. The abandoned clearings are first invaded by three pantropical grasses. Most pervasive of them is the Imperata, which takes over both hill slopes and water clogged areas. The second is wild sugarcane (*Saccharum* sp.), which grows along water courses. Elephant grass (*Miscanthus* sp.) is the third grass which occurs in groves in certain areas. In this way, the Agta primary forest is slowly converted into grassland. Since these grasslands do not contain traditional Agta food resources, the deforestation process effectively reduces the Agta utilized area and, ultimately, the ratio of the human population to resources.

Economic Consequences

The Agta of Isabela in the past lived in a relatively large per capita primary forest area. Notwithstanding the present encroachment, most groups still occupy areas large enough to allow them to continue, partially, their traditional mode of life. However, the continuing trend of encroachment, degradation of the ecosystem and diminution of the area worries most Agta (see Rai 1981), particularly those who still have opted to emphasize the traditional economic system. Moreover, the intensive interaction between the Agta and outside population is leading to competition over some of the same resources. Ultimately, it is resulting in an asymmetrical economic relationship, which is biased against the Agta. In the following pages, I will describe the three negative economic consequences that the Agta are facing today: the relative depletion of their traditional resources; the "niche sharing" with outsiders; and the economic subjugation of the Agta by outsiders.

It will be recalled that the Agta primarily gather their plant resources from the stream vegetation area. The stream vegetation is also the area that is being most seriously affected by the deforestation. For example, one variety of wild yam (*ilus*), which was said to have been abundant along the river terraces and on which particular Agta groups continue to depend during certain months in a year, has been seriously affected by flooding of river terraces or burning of the area for horticultural activity.

Animal resources of the Agta are also adversely affected by the mercantile activities and the expansion of the outside population (Alcala 1976:152–58). The large game animals of the Agta such as pig and deer, called *K-selected species* by animal ecologists, tend to reproduce repeatedly but normally produce only a few offspring at a time, which typically take a long time to mature. For example, particular species of deer, which have a lifespan of up to 20 years (Mech 1979:74), have a low reproductive rate (Hames 1979:248). Particular species of wild pigs (e.g., *Sus scrofa*) have a gestation period of approximately four months and a minimum possible birth interval of eight months. They bear four to five young, which have a low survival rate (Diong 1973:139–41; see also Mudar 1985). Because of their limited offspring and long maturation, the game animals of the Agta are vulnerable to over-exploitation (see also Hayden 1981:525–26). They are also easily affected by disruption of habitat or food chain.

J. Peterson has, however, advanced a contrary argument that the forest encroachment and agricultural expansion into the Agta forest brings positive economic consequences to the Agta (Peterson 1977a, 1977b, 1981; see also Peterson and Peterson 1977). She writes that the contemporary expansion of farmland creates a growing interface of forest and cultivated field. The microhabitat of this interface provides the maximally useful biotope for the wild plants upon which game animals feed (Peterson 1981:20). Thus, the interface between the natural and agricultural land is an optimum environment for game (Peterson 1977a:69). She writes that game is most abundant in this area and it is the "optimal hunting area" for the Agta (Peterson 1978a:9), and that therefore the agricultural expansion creates and maintains an optimal environment for the Agta (1981:15).

Peterson's thesis is primarily based on the traditional ecological hypothesis that the transitional area between two or more diverse plant communities (called *ecotone*) shows a tendency for increased variety and density of plant species (*edge effect*) (Odum 1959:278). The edge effect on plant species, however, still remains a matter of continuing debate in ecology as there is no substantial empirical evidence to prove or disprove it (see Rhoades 1978; Margalef 1968). For animal species, the evidence is even more sketchy. With the exception of a few studies on small animals such as rats (Dwyer 1978), there is no evidence that an ecotone is an optimum feeding area for larger game animals.

For the Agta area, let us assume that the edges between the natural forests and agricultural fields are characterized by an increased diversity of plant species. When an increased diversity of plant species occur in a localized area, individual plant species are usually not clumped but scattered over the area. This suggests that edges such as this are not abundant in plant foods to which animals would be attracted (Rhoades 1978:612; King and Graham 1981:131–32). Further, an ecotone is generally the "tension belt" (Odum 1959:278) and particularly the "artificial" ecotone such as the forest-field edge is ecologically unstable. The forest-field edges are continually disrupted by the agricultural activities of humans and their domestic animals. Therefore, it is very likely that the vegetation at the edge is too poor to attract animals.

We still know too little about the habitat, diet, and feeding behavior of the large game animals of the Agta to make any definitive statement. However, according to the Agta, wild pig and deer are not edge species (see Odum 1959:278), though they are known to visit cultivated fields when certain food crops are standing (e.g., Endicott 1979b:17; Conklin 1959a:60). Informants report that pigs come to eat domestic tubers and deer to eat young leaves of corn and rice. During the crop season, these game animals can damage crops considerably if the farms are not guarded. However, outside of such seasonal visitations these game animals do not frequent the edges.

There are a number of other factors that can discourage the concentration of game animals in the edges of forest and field. Hunting pressure brings dispersal of game populations (Diong 1973:127), and the disruption of the natural habitat due to agricultural activity drives them into distant ranges. That the Agta large game retreat into the interior areas, away from agricultural fields, is suggested by the fact that the Agta prefer to hunt, and that they hunt more productively, in such interior areas (see Mudar 1985:73; Allen 1985:54; Estioko-Griffin 1986:41; Headland 1986:319). A preliminary analysis of ethnobotanical data shows that most food species of the game animals occur in the interior areas of the Agta rain forest. For example, in the case of wild pig, 48% ($N = 88$) of its plant foods are found inside the lowland dipterocarp forest, 45% in other forests such as coastal, montane, and stream vegetation, and only the remaining 7% in the secondary growth vegetation such as landslides and swidden areas. Similarly, 36% of the plant foods of the deer occur in the lowland dipterocarp forest, 55% in other types of forests and only 9% in the secondary vegetation (M. S. Allen, field notes).

Peterson claims that in a particular area in Palanan, approximately 55% of the wild pig and 33% of the deer were killed within 1.5 km of agricultural land clearings (Peterson 1981:10). The other Isabela Agta, who depend on hunting more intensively, on the other hand, claim that hunting is less successful in the agricultural areas. In fact, these groups prefer to camp in areas away from agricultural fields when they are intensively hunting. The Agta groups of the valley watershed depend heavily on hunting, and live an average of 13 km from the nearest agricultural settlements. Only those groups of the coastal areas who depend more heavily on fishing and wage labor rather than hunting live near the agricultural settlements. During a 64-day observation of the hunting activities of a band of Disabungan Agta, the group was observed to live 10 to 16 km from the agricultural settlements and 7 to 13 km from the cultivated fields of the agricultural neighbors. Since they hunted further upriver from the camp, Agta were hunting only in areas which were at least 8 km and often 16 km away from the nearest field of their agricultural neighbors. While there are swidden clearings of the Agta themselves in the upriver areas, the Agta hunted mostly in areas away from such swiddens. During the observation period, 77% of the hunting trips of the Disabungan Agta were made in areas outside the 3-km perimeter of their new and old swiddens (see Appendix 7). Of the 23% of the hunting trips taken within the 3-km perimeter of the swiddens, the majority of them were unsuccessful. Of a total of 35 large game animals killed, only 11% were killed within the 3-km perimeters.

Another negative economic consequence of the expansion of outside populations on the Agta area is the niche-sharing between the Agta and outsiders. In the past, there was little overlapping in the subsistence systems of these two populations. While the small neighboring horticultural populations in the past hunted to supplement their domestic protein sources (as did, occasionally, the agricultural population), the hunting of large wild game was very much an Agta niche. Today, this niche of the Agta is increasingly being encroached on by the outsiders primarily because they have easier access to shotguns. They also use dynamite to kill game animals; they make "pig bombs" by putting explosives inside an edible root and burying it on the rooting area of the pigs. For deer, the bombs are hung on branches of trees. River fishing is another niche increasingly yielding to outsiders' exploitation. The agricultural people use dynamite or electrocution in river fishing. As rivers close to the agricultural settlements become depleted of fish, the outsiders make extended trips to interior areas to exploit the aquatic resources. Agta bands claim that they have to guard the rivers from dynamite, electrocution, or poison fishing by outsiders. In this way, the Agta are being challenged today by outsiders in exploitation of resource niches that were primarily theirs in the past.

The present Agta strategy to counter the increasing competition from the non-Agta populations over their traditional resources has been to intensify their trade of forest products such as copal resin, seashells, rattan, bamboo, and orchids. However, this strategy has its own problems. For example, the market demand for these forest products is unpredictable. In the last two decades, the government has concessionized the extraction and sale of copal resin and rattan and these can be traded only through government-designated contractors. These contractors often fix the price of such products so low that it becomes no longer attractive to collect and sell them.

An even more serious economic worry of the Agta is their increasing dependency on the outsiders. Such a dependency situation has been reported earlier. The Philippine Negrito dependence on their agricultural neighbors has been called parasitism (Kroeber 1928:19), or attributed to *noblesse oblige* on the part of outsiders (Maceda 1964:48). While the agricultural neighbors see things this way, the Agta themselves perceive the opposite; in their view they have been continuously exploited by the outsiders.

The current asymmetrical relationship of the Agta and their neighbors is, in part, based on the economic imbalances between the two populations. J. Peterson (1976) suggests that in the present trade relationship, the economic superiority is in favor of the Agta. She argues that the Agta can provide more goods in trade than the outsiders are willing or able to trade, and thus they can threaten the outsiders by intensifying their trade. She writes that the accelerated trading is a common complaint of outsiders and that they "cohere in the face of mutual threat of Agta economic superiority" (Peterson 1976:329). I have shown above that the Agta do not, and cannot, glut the trade demand of their agricultural neighbors. In fact, they cannot meet it. Therefore, neither the Agta nor outsiders should perceive any economic superiority on the part of the Agta.

My data suggest the symbiosis is biased in favor of the agricultural populations and against the Agta groups (see Griffin 1985a:163; Eder 1988). This bias is rooted in the fact that while the Agta are dependent on the outside agriculturalists for survival, the neighboring agricultural population, on the other hand, could maintain an economic system independent of Agta trade. It is thus an imperative for the Agta to maintain this economic relationship even at the cost of economic exploitation and subordination by outsiders.

The economic exploitation of the Agta by outsiders takes many forms. In the Agta trade of forest items to outsiders, the outsiders fix the price. For example, in spite of the high demand for wild animal protein in the adjoining agricultural settlements, the price of wild animal meat is at least 33 percent lower than for domestic meat. The local dealer who oversees the trade of copal resin and seashells often fixes the price at 20 percent lower than the local market. In other barter trade, Agta are even more exploited. Three to nine wild pigs (approximate value 600 to 2,000 pesos) are demanded in exchange for a second-hand transistor radio (approximate value, 200 pesos). Five hundred pesos worth of tree resin is bartered against an old tape recorder (an approximately 150-peso value). Outsiders justify such transactions by saying that Agta trade goods are wild and so require no work in raising them. Most Agta are unfamiliar with the units of exchange and get further cheated. In wage labor, Agta are often paid less than their agricultural counterparts. Whereas an Agta is hired for only 30 pesos for four days of portering, the help of an outside plowman may cost the Agta as much as half of the production of the field.

Land grabbing by outside agricultural people represents the most serious economic exploitation of certain groups of Agta. As outsiders expand their landholding into the Agta forest, the Agta swiddens are the easiest target. The Agta have neither the means nor intent for legal reprisal. The Philippine land law itself is vague in its stipulation regarding the land rights of indigenous people (see Rice et al. 1973; Rai 1982; Bennagen 1985; Griffin 1985a; Eder 1987). The Agta are thus easily evicted from their holdings (see Maceda 1974:7–8). To avoid confrontation with the encroachers, Agta give up their land claim and move to a new, more remote, area.

The increasing economic relationship between the Agta and outsiders is mainly responsible for bringing consumerism to the Agta. In spite of the fact that the Agta have remained selective in their material desires till today, they spend a considerable proportion of their income from trade and wage labor on consumer goods. Agta today buy items like soap, spices, carbonated drinks, coffee, sugar, canned food, nail polish and face powder. These consumer goods are becoming both a need and a status symbol, particularly to the young Agta. Alcoholism is also rising among the Agta (Turnbull 1930:92; Headland 1986:390–91). They regularly trade a part of their game for commercial liquor and, in the coastal areas, for locally brewed coconut or nipa beverages. The outsiders exploit these acquired habits of the Agta by extending unsolicited credit in the form of consumer goods or beverages to them. Once caught in the downward spiral of indebtedness, Agta can be seriously abused. Often, Agta have left their traditional river valley in order to interrupt any further economic abuse.

The Agta today must devote a considerable amount of their time to nontraditional economic pursuits; consequently they spend proportionately less time foraging. This, and their preference for outside foods and consumer goods, leads to a lesser degree of dependence on the traditional food resources. The two important traditional sources of carboyhydrate food, the wild tuber and caryota palm starch, are exploited less frequently today (see also Allen 1985:56) as they have come to prefer domestic carbohydrates.

The increased dependence of the Agta on the nonforaged foods is reflected in the analysis of their food intake. An energy flow analysis of a band of Disabungan Agta shows that the average daily intake is 2,081 Cal per person per day (see Appendix 11). If one takes into account the individual variations in food consumption and the food consumed outside the camp, the input can be as high as 2,500 Cal per adult per day. Of this total input, the Disabungan Agta derive as much as 60 percent from nontraditional sources (see Appendix 10). It is estimated that some groups of Agta today may derive up to 80 percent of their caloric input from nonforaged foods (see Headland 1986). While the Disabungan Agta consume relatively high amounts of protein and fat (see Appendix 11), the intake may be considerably lower for other Agta groups, who rely more on wage labor or horticulture. If the decrease in the amount of Agta protein intake is very significant, it can affect, among other things, the essential intake of amino acids, which can act as a limiting factor in metabolism (McArthur 1974:114) and can result in malnutrition.

All the Agta groups of northeastern Luzon today experience various degrees of environmental degradation of their forest homeland and economic subjugation by outsiders. One can also confidently predict that this trend is on the increase. There is now growing evidence to indicate that when these conditions are stressful enough, they will have demographic consequences for the Agta. In fact, in a study of the Casiguran Agta, who suffer from serious ecological, economic and social stresses, Headland (1986:381) found that the group had experienced a 40 percent net population decline over a period of half a century due mainly to disease and malnutrition (see also Eder 1987).

Social and Religious Subordination

The Agta are in limbo not only because of their present ecological and economic problems, but also because they are facing a number of changes in their social and symbolic perceptions resulting from their relations with the outsiders. The Agta are being drawn into the social system of the outside population, one they have no control over, and little understanding of.

The evidence that the Agta are experiencing rather rapid disruption in their social system comes from several sources. One indication is the change in their subsistence mode, which has paralleled the change in settlement pattern (see Hart and Pilling 1960; Harako 1976); the constraints imposed by the intensive practice of horticulture and wage labor have brought about a decreased mobility for these Agta groups. There is evidence that the earlier, pervasive role of kinship in the Agta social relations is being de-emphasized. While kinship is the determining factor in the traditional band fission and fusion, the permanent settlement of swidden lands would end these social mechanisms and could require non-kin to live together, thus at times ignoring the traditional rules of residence affiliation.

This Agta shift to nonforaging subsistence and the change in settlement patterns exacts a social price. The economic behavior necessitated by a nonforaging way of life is incompatible with the hunting-gathering custom of sharing; it is a difficult proposition for people who depend on horticulture to share their harvested crops (Lee 1978:7; Cashdan 1980:209). Among the Agta, the more horticulturally oriented groups have begun facing accusation by their more traditional counterparts of untoward hoarding of food items.

A large part of the social and religious changes among the Agta are a result of their social relationships with the outside population. J. Peterson writes that the agricultural neighbors of the Agta are at a disadvantage in their dealings with the spirit world, as they themselves have no healers who can intercede for them (1976:322–29). She claims the skill of the Agta healers in manipulating the shared symbolic world is acknowledged by the non-Agta people who are dependent on the Agta intercession with the spirit world. This "symbolic superiority" of the Agta, according to Peterson, is part of the mechanism for restraining the social and political excesses of the outsiders on the Agta (ibid.:327–29).

On the contrary, I have found that the symbolic realms of the Agta and their agricultural neighbors today have little in common. The Agta do not and cannot manipulate the spiritual world of the outsiders and do not threaten them. Neither the Agta nor the outsiders perceive the spiritual superiority of the Agta and in fact, the reverse is often the case. Thus, the Agta are in no position to restrain the sociopolitical excesses of the outsiders.

The Agta of northeastern Luzon are animists (see Rai 1985). Their supernatural world is an ever-expanding one, where eternal spirits continue to exist and spirits of mortals continue to join them. Agta informants agree that there are two classes of spirits. The first group includes the spirits of deceased humans (*anito*) and the second group represents the eternal animal spirits (*hayup*). The spirits of the deceased humans are usually malignant and malevolent. They insist on continuing to exercise their social relations with the tangible world. If disturbed, they are believed to jinx the living. They are believed to be responsible for causing most spirit-related sicknesses. Because they are also unpredictable, they belong to the most feared category of supernatural spirits. The animal spirits, on the other hand, are generally benevolent. They befriend the Agta shamanistic healers (*bunogen*), who by themselves have no personal constitutional power to heal. With the help of these familiar spirits (called *bunog*), the healers mediate between the living and supernatural worlds.

The traditional version of the Agta animism differs markedly from the folk Christianity of the neighboring agricultural people. It is also different from that of indigenous non-Christian population in the area. For example, Agta animism lacks a sacrificial ceremony. As opposed to other animists in Isabela, Agta do not seem to be concerned about well-being in the afterlife and do not worship any ancestor spirits. In fact, the conjugal pair of dieties, which is so often referred to in the animistic rituals of other Philippine groups (see Scott 1979:99), is unknown to the Agta.

The non-Christian population of Isabela has its own shamanistic healers, who are considered powerful manipulators of the spirit world by both Agta and non-Agta groups. The Christian population does not have shamanistic healers, but has other religious specialists or medicine men (*hérbalaryo*), whose help is sought through offerings and medicines for intervention with the spirit world.

There are a number of myths among the Philippine lowland population regarding the supernatural power of the Negrito groups. One myth about the Negritos claims that they possess a supernatural amulet (I: *anting-anting*), which is said to have the power to make a person invisible. The Agta themselves, while discounting any such supernatural amulet, claim to use some medicinal plants, which are believed to have protective power for the possessor and depotentiating power for an enemy's destructive intentions. The Agta, however, disclaim that they have knowledge of any plant or supernatural object that can inflict harm to others.

Witchcraft and sorcery[1] could be one medium of religious or spiritual manipulation (see Guenther 1976:125; Townsend 1978:293). Among the Agta, witchcraft is acknowledged only in that they believe such power occurs among persons of the non-Agta origin. Sorcery (*ilo*) is claimed to be practiced by a few Agta individuals, who can inflict harm on others, including non-Agta, by manipulating certain objects (Griffin 1984:106). However, all Agta groups in Isabela are unanimous in that they fear more the alleged practice of witchcraft and sorcery among particular non-Agta groups than among themselves.

There are further reasons why the Agta have come to occupy an inferior social and symbolic status in relation to other groups in the area. While the Agta until recently have had only peripheral contact with Christian missionaries (see Headland 1986:197–201; 281–83), today, as with all other non-Christian groups, Agta are coming under the influence of Christianization. Historically, Christianization has had an important sociopolitical meaning for sedentary agricultural people of the Philippines. The groups who accepted colonization and Christianization early in Spanish times and became loyal citizens to the colonial power, were given a higher sociopolitical position. The other groups who resisted colonization and adhered to their indigenous pagan religion were given a respectively lower social position. And, to a large extent, this is still true today.

Among the Isabela populations, the Ilokano, who were among the earliest people to be Christianized by the Spanish, enjoy the highest sociopolitical status. Next in the hierarchy are the indigenous Christian minority groups, who were Christianized later during Spanish times. Among the present day non-Christian groups, the Igorot occupy a higher social position followed by the indigenous horticultural groups (Kalinga); these groups have come into contact with the Christian missionaries since the beginning of this century. Needless to say, the Agta occupy the lowest position in the local sociopolitical hierarchy.

Supported by the demographic dominance and the political structure of the area, the social ranking of the groups is understood and more or less accepted by all groups.

Reflecting this hierarchy, the women from socially inferior groups prefer to enter a hypergamous unions with men of socially higher status; for example, women from the horticultural group prefer to marry men from the agricultural group. Following the pattern, Agta women from particular groups have recently shown preference to marry men from horticultural as well as agricultural groups (see Headland 1986:371). While their inferior social status is one primary reason why the Agta women marry men from the agricultural or horticultural populations, it may also be partly due to their inferior economic status (see Speth n.d.b; cf. Bailey 1985). Notwithstanding the practice of hypergamy, the different groups of people in Isabela see themselves as distinct, and generally the higher ranking groups tend to ostracize the subordinate groups socially, politically, and economically. For the Agta, their animistic religion, their foraging economy (which does not allow wealth accumulation), their distinct Negrito physical features and their lack of political power reinstate their social position at the bottom of the hierarchy.

To conclude, the analysis of the Agta transitional world indicates that the once socioeconomically independent Agta groups have become economically interdependent with (and more recently, totally dependent on) the neighboring agricultural and horticultural populations in the last two centuries. The external encroachment and the subsequent changes created by it, played a role in bringing about the shift away from a traditional to a transitional system. While Agta groups did participate differentially, the trend was to increasingly incorporate the nonforaging economic strategies of external trade, horticulture and wage labor. The continuing interaction with and encroachment by agricultural and mercantile populations are causing the Agta to experience environmental degradation of their area, as well as economic, social, and religious subjugation by the outsiders. These various conditions, processes and consequences have brought about the present change among the Agta. If the traditional Agta world was characterized by the forest orientation and socioeconomic egalitarianism, their transitional world today is characterized by an increasing dependence on the outside world and its concomitant social costs.

PART IV

CONCLUSIONS

11
Summary

This study of the Agta Negritos of northeastern Luzon was carried out with two primary goals. First, it was carried out to document the ethnography of the hunting and gathering Agta society. Second, it attempted to analyze the conditions, processes, and consequences of the Agta change from a traditional forest-oriented way of life to a transitional one, where foraging is combined with nonforaging strategies to make a living. This chapter summarizes the findings and major conclusions and suggests the wider theoretical and substantive significance of the present work.

The physical environment of the various groups of the Agta of northeastern Luzon is a rugged terrain: a continuous chain of predominantly lowland dipterocarp forest interrupted only by the river system. Depending on the area, the Agta groups operate in rain forest areas approximately 2 to 5 km^2 per capita. The relatively stable tropical vegetative community is marked by a very high species diversity. The Agta, who realize the constraints of their ecosystem, exploit the interior forests mostly for terrestrial animal resources; stream vegetation areas mostly for plant resources; and rivers, lagoons and sea for aquatic resources. Notwithstanding the minor variations across the two watersheds of the Sierra Madre range, the Agta rain forest area experiences rather consistently high temperature, rainfall and humidity all throughout the year. In spite of the fact that there is not a marked ecological seasonality in the environment, Agta distinguish between the "wet" period of the northeast monsoon and the "dry" period of the southwest monsoon.

Due to the nonseasonal environment, and to their dependence on a nexus of plant and animal resources at any given time, the Agta experience little seasonal scarcity of the traditional resources. They cope with the short-term fluctuations in resources by making adjustments in their subsistence strategies and settlement pattern.

The traditional sociocultural environment of the Agta is complex but well defined. Kinship is the primary organizing principle. In the bilateral kinship system of the Agta, all members of society are categorized by an individual into two exclusive groups, namely, kin and non-kin. With a few exceptions, marriage is forbidden with all kin by a strict incest rule. Non-kin are potential marriage partners but, until and unless such a marital link is formed, they are distrusted and avoided in socioeconomic interactions.

The regional Agta population of Isabela is divided into four linguistic groups, occupying adjacent and roughly rectangular forest areas along the north-south axis of the Sierra Madre range. A linguistic group is not a political or defense unit and does not see itself as territorial in its control of a homeland and exploitation of resources. However, since each linguistic group is generally endogamous, and because cross-linguistic group marriages are rare, a linguistic group in itself represents the maximal extent of the kinship network. And because members of another linguistic group are non-kin and therefore strongly avoided in social relations, each linguistic group maintains its socioeconomic isolation from another. In the past, this socioeconomic isolation was reinforced by the occasional practice of interlinguistic raiding. Today, the allegations and suspicion of such practices keep the linguistic groups socially apart.

A linguistic group occupies an area which usually extends to both watersheds of the Sierra Madre range. While extensive social ties are regularly maintained among members of a linguistic group living across the watershed, the greater physical distance involved forces them to interrupt regular economic ties. Thus a linguistic group is divided into two economically independent watershed groups. While Agta members can reside anywhere within a linguistic area, a watershed group remains fairly circumscribed. Within the watershed group, the members maintain more intensive social interactions and a more efficient communication network. Within a watershed group, the Agta are divided into various river valley groups. A river valley group is composed of a population of stable core members who maintain even closer socioeconomic ties among themselves. It is also the socioresidential unit that Agta members tend to most closely identify themselves with.

A river valley group is further divided into bands. The bands camp along the river terrace or beach in an average of four to five kilometers distance from one another. Averaging 21 people, a band is the minimal economically viable unit. Since a kin relationship is required for band membership, a band tends to be made up of closely related kin. As the kinship network of the band changes through new marital alliances or the death of members, the band composition becomes fluid, allowing the fusion of members who are kin and the fission of those who have become non-kin. The band formation of the Agta is a direct response to their kinship network (and not necessarily a response to the resource distribution of their physical environment).

Within a band, families are the smallest residential units. Predominantly of the nuclear type, families maintain their own lean-tos and hearths, and are the decision-making units of the Agta. For particular couples or families, long-term residence rules are jurally given. The newlyweds must reside with wife's close kin until the bride service obligation is completed and those remarried couples reside with the husband's kin. Others can exercise a number of options in their long-term residence affiliations but choose close kin in actual residence affiliations.

Against these backgrounds of physical and social environments, the traditional Agta economy is oriented towards the forest. In the past, the Agta exploited their traditional forest resources by foraging—primarily by hunting, and secondarily by gathering and fishing. Today, while groups of Agta vary in their degree of dependence on these three foraging strategies, they remain first and foremost hunters who derive only secondary subsistence from gathering and fishing. Agta ethnozoology recognizes three life forms among terrestrial animals ("walking animals," "crawling animals" and "flying animals"). While the inventory of game animals includes members from the three life forms and includes six species of mammals, two reptiles and various species of birds, the wild pig and deer are the major game animals of the Agta. Using only bow and arrow (and dogs), the Agta make use of five hunting strategies (searching, hiding, trailing, ambushing and cornering) and a number of collective and individual techniques. Today, particular groups of Agta spend as much as 48 percent of their working time in hunting-related activities and derive 23 percent of their total caloric intake directly from the consumption of wild animal meat.

Gathering of plant resources and honey is a secondary, and opportunistic, activity of the Agta. They categorize plants into three life forms: "grasses," "vines" and "trees." Of the several hundred plants Agta recognize, fewer than three hundred have direct economic use or symbolic value to the group and fewer than fifty are food species. Of the food species, varieties of wild tubers, rattan, wild fruits and vegetables are most regularly exploited. Following the recent Agta dependence on cultivated foods, which are acquired mainly through trade, gathering of plant foods have been de-emphasized. Aquatic resources such as fish, eel or octopus are exploited in varying degrees by the Agta. Traditionally, these three foraging activities provided the Agta with a consistently reliable livelihood in their rain forest homeland.

The Agta use a number of sociocultural mechanisms to insure a predictable resource return. Since the plant resources are scattered throughout the rain forest, the Agta must be highly mobile to exploit them. Camp moves are as frequent as twenty times a year, a mobility pattern which puts little stress on resource locales and favors the sustainability of the ecosystem. Because the Agta do not observe taboos, either of particular wild food species or methods of exploitation, all culturally known resources can be exploited uninterruptedly. The Agta have a flexible sexual divison of labor, and thus they are able to make efficient use of everyone's skill and energy to offset their technological limitations. More importantly, the egalitarian Agta practice sharing of acquired foods; they allocate meat and other procured foods equally to families within a band. Sharing provides regular access to a variety of diets. It also allocates food in small but regular amounts per individual, and thus brings efficient consumption and metabolism of food items.

Given their diversified nexus of resource bases and the numerous mechanisms of resource exploitation and allocation, one would have expected the numerically small Agta population to continue to subsist by foraging alone. Moreover, analysis of past Agta demography indicates that their past population trend was probably marked by a relatively low fertility rate. Probably because the causes of Agta deaths were also few, the mortality rate was also low. Under these conditions, the Agta population in the past experienced only a small growth rate. Analysis of the population-to-resources ratio further reveals that the Agta lived at levels below the carrying capacity of their environment. Even if a low population growth resulted in a decreased ratio of certain resources to the Agta, they successfully coped by intensifying their traditional mechanisms, either economic or sociocultural.

The Agta way of life was disrupted by upheavals for which they were not responsible. Attracted primarily by the prospect of tobacco cash-cropping, large-scale immigration was taking place in the adjacent lowland agricultural basin. The immigrants brought with them sophisticated agricultural technology and aggressive land tenure systems. These immigrants displaced the politically weaker indigenous horticultural people who were, in turn, forced to relocate in the Agta homelands. While some Agta groups adjusted by retreating further into interior areas, many were forced to adjust by adapting new, nonforaging economic strategies.

To make matters worse, the Agta forest home became the target of commercial logging, particularly since the 1950s. Having access to the regional highway and with leftover machinery from World War II, the logging companies extracted large amounts of timber. In the following decade, mining companies entered the area. The incursion of the mercantile groups was radically different from the earlier encroachment of the agricultural population; while agricultural expansion was concentrated mostly in the forest fringes along the low-lying river terraces, the mercantile activities exploited the high canopy interior forest. These industries, which depended on outside skilled laborers, encouraged further immigration of outsiders. By removing big trees from the forest and by opening up the forest with logging trails, they created ideal situations for further agricultural expansion. The later immigrants often pioneered directly into the middle of the forest, establishing colonies of agricultural people in the Agta homeland.

The encroachment acted as a catalyst for other changes in the traditional Agta world. For example, the Agta experienced intensive contact with a multi-ethnic and polyglot population. The net immigration of outside populations raised the population density of the area many-fold. Mercantile encroachment and subsequent agricultural expansion affected the original ratio of the Agta to their resources. This multiplicity of factors provided the major impetus for dramatic change among the Agta.

The presence of a large agricultural and mercantile population in the Agta forest home encouraged the Agta to de-emphasize foraging subsistence and take up new economic pursuits. They accelerated their trade of forest items, particularly the meat of wild animals and fish. As the volume of their trade increased so did their reliance on, and taste for, cultivated cereals. In particular areas, Agta entered into institutionalized trade partnerships with outsiders in order to obtain regular supplies of domestic cereals. Today, when Agta continue to experience an increasing deficit of domestic cereals, they increasingly trade their animal protein to meet this deficit.

To supplement the import of domesticated cereals, Agta also are increasingly engaging in horticulture. They clear forests along river terraces in small patches. Closely related kin in one band will clear a cluster of gardens in an area and practice a long fallow cycle of shifting cultivation to plant mainly upland rice, corn, sweet potato and cassava. The practice of horticulture, however, remains erratic as families tend not to plant crops every year, and the yield also remains low.

Following the development of intensive Agta-outsider relationships, the Agta were drawn into, and in some cases pushed into, the practice of wage labor. Today, they work as porters and laborers for outside agricultural people and as guides and guards for mercantile people. A few Agta bands, who live close to agricultural settlements, have become largely dependent on this nonforaging activity. Depending on the locally available economic opportunities, the Agta groups of Isabela vary in their adoption of these new, nonforaging economic strategies. Agta bands who have largely de-emphasized foraging may derive up to 80 percent of their subsistence from wage labor.

The consequences of the external encroachment as well as the increased dependency of the Agta on outsiders are numerous and generally negative. The rampant exploitation of the forest for agricultural and mercantile purposes has initiated both qualitative and quantitative changes in the rain forest ecosystem. The continuing perturbation of the forest ecosystem adversely affects the plant and animal resources of the Agta. The increasing trend of deforestation and thus diminution of Agta forest homeland lowers the ratio of traditional resources to Agta. Further, the outside population is increasingly competitive with the Agta to exploit what were traditionally Agta resources. Over-exploitation of these resources by outsiders is bringing about their depletion. To offset the declining return from traditional resources, Agta are intensifying the exploitation and trade of other forest and marine items such as copal resin, rattan, seashells, and orchids. However, because the market demand of these trade items is unpredictable and because the dealers often fix prices at a level much below market value, this trade is often unattractive.

The one-way dependency of Agta on outsiders has brought about an economically biased relationship whereby the outsiders exploit the Agta. Because the Agta are unfamiliar with units of exchange and have little knowledge of arithmetic, they often are further cheated. Not infrequently, Agta are caught in a downward spiral of indebtedness to outsiders and are further abused by demands on their labor. The Agta swiddens are the first target for land-grabbing and agricultural expansion. Because they have neither the means nor intent for legal reprisal, the Agta are pre-empted from their land.

The ecological and economic problems of the Agta have parallel consequences in their sociocultural realms. In their intensive interaction with outsiders, the Agta are experiencing changes in their traditional sociocultural system. The traditional importance of kinship in residence affiliation must be overlooked as they come together to pursue wage labor. Camp movement is similarly hindered by the constraints of swiddening as well as intensive trading of commercial forest items.

The asymmetrical economic relations of the Agta is reflected in their biased socio-symbolic position vis-à-vis the outsiders. To the agricultural people, who define social position on the basis of technological levels and the degree of Christianization, the Agta occupy the lowest position in the social hierarchy. In order to help offset the social dominance of the outsiders, and perhaps to alleviate some of the symbolic anxieties, the Agta are trying their best to emulate the outsiders. They imitate outsiders often by dissociating themselves from the traditional Agta way of life. But because their contrasting physical features are distinctive, they remain alienated from the outside social mainstream and continue to occupy a socially and symbolically subordinate position.

In conclusion, the wider theoretical and substantive significance of this study must be pointed out. In spite of dramatic changes in their life style in recent years, the Agta remain the most traditional foraging group of the Philippine Negritos and represent one of the few surviving hunter-gatherer societies in Asia. An ethnographic undertaking among hunter-gatherers like the Agta, whose culture is rapidly disappearing today, is first of all a contribution to hunter-gatherer studies and, more generally to the ethnological literature. This study is not, however, simply a "salvage" ethnography; it has wider theoretical applications with respect to understanding human societies and how they change.

This study has aimed at a systemic analysis of the Agta traditional system and its change. In accordance with the theory that a society will maintain or change itself in a holistic manner, this study has emphasized the ecological, economic and sociocultural realms of the traditional and transitional systems of the Agta. Similarly, a multitude of systemic reciprocities within and between the physical and sociocultural components of the Agta system have been analyzed.

This study also makes a conscious effort to distinguish between the investigator's and the insider's understandings of the Agta world. Descriptions of the various aspects of the Agta are supported or supplemented by the analysis of folk taxonomies, and terminologies as well as the verbal appraisal of the informants themselves. Additionally, this study integrates in its analysis different mid-level theories and concepts from various traditionally non-anthropological fields of study.

This study of social change illuminates the mechanisms of transformation of the technologically simple societies of the world. While the degree and nature of transformation in human societies vary, the basic principles by which these societies change are cross-cultural. They all change due to complex conditions, by systemic processes and often with unanticipated but dramatic consequences. These basic principles are easily discernible in a study of change among technologically simple hunter-gatherers like the Agta. It is hoped that this study will add a new dimension to a cross-cultural model of change in human societies.

12
The Agta Future

For the Agta, the present environmental, economic, and social and symbolic problems that face them are dramatic. They are coping with these conditions as best as they can by a compromise between traditional and nontraditional strategies. Simply put, the Agta are becoming too dependent to stand on their own. One would expect that such a situation, as well as the perception by outsiders that Agta are socially inferior, would necessarily create apprehension among the Agta. At a very human level, the Agta dilemma is to try to reconcile themselves to what they have become, particularly to their loss of economic autonomy with its accompanying negative consequences.

This anthropological study has concluded that the root cause of the Agta problems, in the past and today, lies in the outside intervention in their system. The present trend indicates that the external encroachment on the Agta rain forest home will continue at an accelerated pace in the future. Thus, it is very likely that the transformation of the Agta traditional world will also continue at an accelerated pace.

Although it is desirable, one does not expect countries like the Philippines to put a complete ban on mercantile operations in forest areas like that of the Agta. Larger national interests have always threatened to undermine any desire to protect indigenous peoples and their cultures. Forest-related industries are the source of much needed foreign exchange. They also provide employment and vital raw materials for domestic consumption. These short-term economic benefits outweigh any long-term ecological considerations pertaining to the mercantile activities.

The encroachment of the Agta forest home by the agricultural population will also continue. The agricultural immigrants are encroaching on the Agta forest areas for reasons of compulsion rather than choice; they are escaping the conditions of overpopulation and underproduction in their places of origin. The frontier may be crowded by Agta standards, but it is still vast and empty by agricultural standards, and immigrants go there to take refuge. Frontier immigration is not simply a matter of economics. It is also a reminder of political upheavals elsewhere; the Huk Rebellion that erupted in the Central Luzon Plains in the early half of this century resulted in the mass emigration of an allegedly dissident population (Kirkvliet 1979). Some of the immigrants to the Agta homeland, such as those from the Central Cordillera, are themselves victims of an earlier environmental degradation of their home area; they were forced to immigrate to these frontiers after their area was destroyed by deforestation, siltation or inundation.

While the future of the traditional Agta way of life hinges very much on the discontinuation of the external incursions on their homeland, they do not, and will not, in any foreseeable set of circumstances, have the power to stop this encroachment. Typical of hunter-gatherers, the Agta are politically a very fragmented group. They have no loyalty beyond the kin group and no ties of alliance to extra-linguistic groups. Such political organization, or the absence of it, cripples the ability of the Agta to form a united front and thus pose any political threat to outsiders. As a result, they do not have the political clout needed to discourage the course of mercantile or agricultural expansion in their homeland.

How then will the Agta cope in the future? What economic choices do the Agta have and how will these choices determine future changes? What parallel or subsequent sociocultural changes must the Agta seek? If one could assume that the principles on which the Agta system maintains and changes itself today would remain operative in the future too, one would foresee a continued compromise between traditional and nontraditional economic strategies. This option for the sake of economic survival will require a further shift away from the traditional Agta structure, organization, values and norms.

The Agta could further intensify their traditional sociocultural mechanisms to counter the declining return of their traditional resources. For example, increased camp mobility to exploit the depleting resources could bring a better return of their traditional resources. The problem, however, is that increased mobility is already constrained by factors which are not conducive to nomadism such as their practice of horticulture and wage labor. Or, the Agta could borrow more modern technology. Shotguns and dynamite would probably allow greater exploitation of their traditional animal resources. However, the intensive use of technology can bring about the total depletion of the resources themselves.

Intensification of trade with outsiders has often been a preferred strategy of economically marginal people to offset their declining resources (Murphy and Steward 1956). Among the traditional foraging people of the Philippines, the intensive trade of copal resin by the Batak, who derive approximately one-third of their total caloric intake from it (Eder 1978:59), is the best example. For the Agta too, a further intensification of their trade with outsiders could be one of their future economic alternatives for solving their continuing economic undersufficiency. One can safely assume that the market for the meat of wild animals will not decline in the foreseeable future, given that the agricultural and mercantile populations will continue to rise. The Agta could also continue to intensify their trade of copal resin, rattan, and seashells. The only problem with intensive exploitation of these resources could again be the depletion of these commercial resources.

The Agta could escape from contributing directly to the degradation of their ecosystem if they were to take particular kinds of wage employment. For example, intensive dependence on the practice of agricultural labor for domestic cereals could be a way to make up their carbohydrate deficit without contributing to the environmental degradation. It must, however, be recalled that this opportunity is available only during the agricultural harvest season. Furthermore, the Agta ultimately could lose this employment when the agricultural homesteaders themselves reach a point of underemployment.

The intensification of trade and wage labor as long-term economic pursuits could bring about more serious problems. These options would probably mean that the Agta would become further dependent on outsiders. This could bring about spiraling indebtedness and further economic exploitation. Particular Agta groups, who have chosen to depend on wage labor alone, have entered a state of near servitude with outsiders, and other groups are becoming equally vulnerable to socioeconomic subjugation.

Since the above-mentioned economic options of the Agta create a number of problems, to pursue any single one would not be an optimal long-term response of the Agta. The Agta themselves seem to be aware of the fact that choosing only one or a few options is a risky proposition and that holding onto all options is the only insurance for the future.

Specialization in a particular economic resource is also against the traditional economic norm of hunter-gatherers like the Agta. Because they exploit and depend on broad-spectrum resource bases, the traditional exploitative strategy of the Agta is that of the generalist; they exploit a wide range of resources, including the less preferred ones, to insure a predictable return. Economically, the Agta groups are also opportunists in the sense that they switch their course of action to take advantage of available opportunities. Therefore, it is probable that the Agta will choose to practice a compromise economic subsistence that will combine both traditional and nontraditional strategies.

The present indications are, however, such that within the general framework of the Agta economics of flexibility, horticulture will probably occupy the pivotal position. That is, as hunting in the past, and trade today, play the important role, horticulture will probably be the most consistent activity with which the future economy of the Agta will be identified and on which other economic activities will be orchestrated.

To say that horticulture will be the pivotal economic activity of the Agta in the future is not to say that its practice does not face problems. For one, the outside population may prevent, or at least delay, the Agta from moving into such a horticultural niche by aggressively taking over the accessible lands (see Headland 1986:404). One can only say that the pursuit of horticulture will probably be the best option available to them. Aside from agricultural and household wage labor, horticulture is the alternative that would be least affected by the environmental degradation of the Agta forests: as long as there is land area to allow an appropriate swidden cycle, it can have long-term sustainability. Unlike trade and wage labor, horticulture allows the Agta to de-emphasize their undesirable economic dependence on outsiders, and to escape the socioeconomic dominance of outsiders.

A successful adaptation to a non-forest-based economy, particularly horticulture, can take place only when there are concomitant changes in the sociocultural realms. Often these shifts mean accepting not only alien ideological concepts but also accepting conditions that are inherently contradictory to the traditional ones. Such economic changes thus can be costly to societies like the Agta. While the Agta probably would experience problems in a number of areas, they will surely face contradictions in three particular shifts; namely, settlement pattern, concept of property, and resource allocation.

Mobility is crucial to the Agta, who have traditionally used space extensively. Understandably, it is part of the "fabric of Agta culture" (W. Peterson 1981:51), and "second nature to the Agta" (Bennagen 1977:188). While the Agta bands traditionally move among numerous campsites, increased dependence on horticulture will enforce considerably lower mobility than hunting and gathering.

The trend toward sedentism among the Agta can also lead to other sociopolitical incompatibilities. For example, in the event that the kinship network changes, the families today can quickly and easily alternate their residence affiliation. They will lose this luxury once they have to live in a relatively permanent settlement and in permanent houses. It is possible that the Agta will not be able to maintain social cohesion in large settlements where both kin and non-kin must live together. These factors explain why the resettlement efforts among the Agta by the government agencies have consistently failed.

An emphasis on horticulture by hunter-gatherers like the Agta is also likely to require a shift in the concept of private property. Traditionally, the Agta have a poorly developed concept of ownership of their estate or material possessions. Because of this, the Agta are easily pre-empted by the outsiders, particularly the agricultural population. Thus, the Agta themselves have begun claiming long-term rights to their swidden land. This shift from a norm where the concept of private property was absent to one where it is deemed essential introduces a number of incompatibilities. Agta ownership and permanent occupation of swidden land will no doubt inhibit their foraging patterns.

Another fundamental distinction between the hunter-gatherers and horticulturalists is in their allocation of resources. The Agta, like most other hunter-gatherers, regard saving and surfeit accumulation as hoarding with all its pejorative connotations (Sahlins 1965:215–18). Thus, they share food, including harvested crops. The sharing norm is generally de-emphasized among horticultural people, whose reciprocity is structured on a *quid pro quo* basis. Among them, saving is valued as the Agta value sharing. If Agta were to begin saving, they would then be caught between the effects of social pressure forcing them to an immediate expenditure of surplus and their recognition of the possible transformation of surfeit to saving (Peterson 1978a:111). Since sharing is an important traditional means of resource allocation among the Agta today, the practice of saving could bring economic and nutritional disruptions.

In conclusion, the future economic survival of the Agta will depend on their successful incorporation of nonforaging economic strategies. As these new economic pursuits bring their own constellation of values, beliefs and constraints that are often in conflict with the old order, the Agta will surely incur heavy organizational costs. In the long run, to survive, and to survive as a distinct group, the Agta society must be able to reconcile the various strains of dissonance.

Notes

CHAPTER 1
1. The Negritos of the Philippines are variously called by themselves, or by their neighbors, Agta, Aeta, Ayta, or Ata. These are proto-Austronesian words for "a Negrito person" (see Headland 1986:2, 175).

CHAPTER 3
1. When asked for Agta census records, Philippine municipal and barrio officials reported that the Agta are considered transients and thus were not included in the national or local census.

CHAPTER 4
1. A number of the botanical names were furnished by Dr. Domingo Madulid, Curator of the Philippine National Herbarium, on the basis of plant collections by the author.
2. There is disagreement as to whether or not the northeastern Luzon experiences ecological seasonality (see Griffin 1984:98–99 for review; see also Estioko-Griffin 1984:54–62; Allen 1985:47–48).

CHAPTER 5
1. J. Peterson (1977a:117) writes that among the Agta, the child of one's parent's older sibling is addressed as "older sibling" irrespective of the "child's" age. However, in my study, I found that it is the age of the child relative to the other individual, rather than the sibling order of their parents, that is the determining factor of this Agta kinship term.
2. *Band* often carries a connotation of territorial ownership, corporateness and fixed membership (Woodburn 1968b:103). This connotation does not apply to the Agta bands. The Agta word *pisan* has often been used to mean band (e.g., Bennagen 1969a:5–7; Peterson 1978a). My information is that Agta use this word only as a verb (*magpisan*) to mean "to come together or to be together" (see also Headland et al. 1974:122).
3. The flow chart is a working model of the Agta residence choices, and thus has been kept general. Short visits or temporary residences are not accounted for in the chart. It was found that the accuracy rate of the chart is higher when applied to more forest-oriented Agta groups.

CHAPTER 6
1. *Working time* is defined here as a span of time from the beginning to the end of a specific activity. *Hunting time* means the period that is spent away from the camp for the purpose of hunting, although other activities may be carried out during this time.

CHAPTER 7
1. There are no meteorological data presently available from the Palanan Bay area. The Casiguran Bay area, which lies approximately 100 km south of the Palanan Bay and has similar

orographic features, shows no marked dry and wet seasons. Even in the driest month, the mean monthly rainfall is 166 mm. The temperature fluctuates by only 4° C from the coldest (January) to the hottest (June) month (Flores et al. 1969:176–84).
2. While the Agta have no specific names for such groups, they identify such groups with names of particular rivers or other geographical reference points in the area. I have done the same in the text.

CHAPTER 8

1. While the debate is far from settled, most anthropologists believe that in prehistoric times, the transition from Pleistocene to Archaic/Mesolithic (see Hayden 1981) or to Neolithic cultures (Howell 1976:138) cannot be linked to internal population pressures resulting from population growth.
2. The term *agriculture* is used in this book to mean cultivation of permanent fields, while *horticulture* is used to mean the cultivation of temporary, and usually small, field plots such as in swidden cultivation. Philippine lowland societies such as the Ilokano practice agriculture, and the later immigrants to the area in question, deriving from these societies, are therefore referred to as *agricultural groups*. Other ethnic groups that have been settled in this area for some time derive their livelihood primarily from swidden farming and are, therefore, referred to here as *horticultural groups*. As will be seen, the Agta also practice horticulture on occasion, but they are not what I call a "horticultural group" because they do not depend on it as a primary subsistence strategy.
3. The Kalinga horticulturists described in this text have no known tribal or linguistic connection with the western Luzon groups of the same name (see Scott 1979:93). The term *kalinga*, which literally means "enemy" in many north Luzon languages, was applied to all non-Christian people inhabiting areas in and around the Cagayan Valley.

CHAPTER 9

1. In the barrio of Del Pilar, San Mariano Municipality, where the Disabungan Agta trade, the agricultural families keep an average of two chickens (or ducks) per household, and one pig and one dog (which is eaten) per every two households (MDS 1979:31).
2. Among the game animals killed by the Disabungan Agta, the male adult wild pig weighed, on the average, 30 kg ($N = 8$); the female adult, 23 kg ($N = 9$); and the young adult, 17 kg ($N = 12$). Of the deer, the average buck weighed 32 kg ($N = 4$); the doe, 25 kg ($N = 6$); and the young adult, 11 kg ($N = 5$).
3. When metabolized, .25 to .33 kg of meat will supply an individual's daily protein requirement (see Appendix 9), which is approximately 30 grams (see McArthur 1974:114).

CHAPTER 10

1. *Witchcraft* is defined here as that destructive power that is rooted in the individual's own resources. *Sorcery* is that power of an individual which derives from the utilization of resources external to the individual, such as magical procedures (Lieban 1967:65).

References Cited

Aiyappan, A.
    1948   Report on the Socio-Economic Conditions of the Aboriginal Tribes of the Province of Madras. Madras: The Government Press.

Alcala, A. C.
    1976   Philippine Land Vertebrates. Quezon City: New Day Publishers

Allen, M. S.
    1985   The rain forest of northeast Luzon and Agta foragers. In: The Agta of Northeastern Luzon: Recent Studies, P. Bion Griffin and A. Estioko-Griffin (eds.). Cebu City: University of San Carlos.

Anderson, J. A.
    1973   Ecological anthropology and anthropological ecology. In: Handbook of Social and Cultural Anthropology, J. J. Honigmann (ed.). Chicago: Rand McNally College.

Andres, S.
    1980   Les Negritos des Philippines: L'apprentissage de la sedentarité. Sudestasie, 2:55–56.

Antonio, L. R.
    1974   Geology and Mineral Resources of Isabela Province. Manila: Bureau of Mines.

Appell, G. N. (ed.)
    1976   The Societies of Borneo. Washington: American Anthropological Association.

Bailey, R. C.
    1985   The Socioecology of Efe Pygmy Men in the Ituri Forest, Zaire. Ph.D. dissertation. Harvard University. (Forthcoming publication of the Museum of Anthropology, University of Michigan.)

Balikci, A.
    1970   The Netsilik Eskimo. New York: The Natural History Press.

Barbosa, A.
    1985   The ethnography of the Agta of Lamika, Peñablanca, Cagayan. In: The Agta of Northeastern Luzon: Recent Studies, P. Bion Griffin and A. Estioko-Griffin (eds.). Cebu City: University of San Carlos.

Barrera, A.
    1969   Soil Survey of Isabela Province. Manila: Bureau of Printing.

Barrows, D. P.
    1908   Eighth Annual Report of the Director of Education. Manila: Bureau of Printing.

Barth F.
1966 Models of Social Organization. Occasional Paper 23. London: Royal Anthropological Institute.

1967 On the study of social change. American Anthropologist, 69(6):661–69.

Barton, R. F.
1946 The Religion of the Ifugaos. Memoir 65. Washington: American Anthropological Association.

Baumgartner, J.
1975 Some remarks on the problem of the Negrito language(s). Philippine Quarterly of Culture and Society, 3:283-85.

Bennagen, P. L.
1969a The Agta of Palanan, Isabela: Surviving food-gatherers, hunters, and fishermen. Esso Silangan, XIV(3):5–7.

1969b Becoming an anthropologist: Fieldwork among the Agta of Palanan, Isabela. In: Anthropology: Range and Relevance, M. Zamora (ed.). Quezon City: Kayumanggi Publishers.

1976 Kultura at Kapaligiran: Pankulturang Pagbabao at Kapanatagan an mga Agta sa Palanan, Isabela. Master's thesis. The University of the Philippine System, Quezon City.

1977 The Negrito: A rallying call to save a Filipino group from cultural extinction. In: Filipino Heritage: The Making of a Nation, A. Roces (ed.). Manila: Lahing Filipino Publishing Co.

1985 Philippines: Swidden cultivation among the Dumagat. In: Swidden Cultivation in Asia. Vol. 3. Bangkok: UNESCO

Bennett, J. W.
1969 Northern Plainsmen: Adaptive Strategy and Agrarian Life. Chicago: Aldine Publishing Co.

1976a The Ecological Transition: Cultural Anthropology and Human Adaptation. New York: Pergman Press.

1976b Anticipation, adaptation, and concept of culture in anthropology. Science, 192(4242):847–53.

Berlin, B.
1978 Ethnobiological classification. In: Cognition and Categorization, E. Rosch and B. Lloyd (eds.). Hillsdale, N. J.: Lawrence Erlbaum Associates.

BFD (Bureau of Forestry Development)
1977 Philippine Forestry Statistics. Manila: Bureau of Forestry Development.

Binford, L. R.
1968a Methodological considerations of the archeological use of ethnographic data. In: Man the Hunter, R. B. Lee and I. DeVore (eds.). Chicago: Aldine Publishing Co.

1968b Post-Pleistocene adaptations. In: New Perspective in Archeology, S. R. Binford and L. R. Binford (eds.). Chicago: Aldine Publishing Co.

1980 Willow smoke and dogs' tails: Hunter-gatherer settlement systems and archeological site formation. American Antiquity, 45(1):4–20.

Birdsell, J. B.
1957 Some population problems involving Pleistocene man. Cold Spring Harbor Symposia on Quantitative Biology, 22:47–68.

Blair, E. H., and J. A. Robertson (eds.)
1903 The Philippine Islands, 1493–1898. 55 Vols. Cleveland: Arther H. Clark Co.
–09

Bodley, J. H.
1975 Victims of Progress. California: Cumming Publishing Co.

Bohannan, P. J.
1971 The impact of money on an African subsistence economy. In: Conformity and Conflict: Readings in Cultural Anthropology, J. P. Spradley and D. W. McCurdy (eds.). Boston: Little, Brown, and Company.

1980 You can't do nothing. American Anthropologist, 82(3):508–24.

Boserup, E.
1965 The Conditions of Agricultural Growth: The Economics of Agrarian Change Under Population Pressure. Chicago: Aldine Publishing Co.

Boulding, K. E.
1956 The Image. Ann Arbor: University of Michigan Press.

Brosius, J. P.
1981 After Duwagan: Deforestation, Succession, and Adaptation in Upland Luzon, Philippines. Master's thesis. The University of Hawaii, Honolulu.

1983 The Zambales Negritos: Swidden agriculture and environmental change. Philippine Quarterly of Culture and Society, 11(2–3):123–48.

Brown, W. H., and D. M. Mathews
1914 Philippine dipterocarp forests. Philippine Journal of Science, IX(5):413–543.

Brush, S. B.
1975 The concept of carrying capacity for systems of shifting cultivation. American Anthropologist, 77:799–811.

Bryant, J. P.
1981 Hare trigger. Natural History, 90(11):46–53.

Buchler, I. R., and H. A. Selby
1968 Kinship and Social Organization: An Introduction to Theory and Method. New York: The Macmillan Company.

Buckley, W.
1967 Sociology and Modern Systems Theory. Englewood Cliffs: Prentice Hall.

1968 Society as a complex adaptive system. In: Modern Systems Research for the Behavioral Scientist, W. Buckley (ed.). Chicago: Aldine Publishing Co.

Cadeliña, R. V.
 1974 Notes on beliefs and practices of contemporary Negritos and the extent of their integration with the lowland Christians in southern Negros. Philippine Quarterly of Culture and Society, 2:47–60.

 1982 Batak Interhousehold Food Sharing: A Systematic Analysis of Food Management of Marginal Agriculturalists in the Philippines. Ph.D. dissertation. The University of Hawaii, Honolulu.

 1988 A comparison of Batak and Ata subsistence styles in two different social and physical environments. In: Ethnic Diversity and the Control of Natural Resources in Southeast Asia, A. T. Rambo, K. Gillogly and K. L. Hutterer (eds.). Center for South and Southeast Asian Studies. The University of Michigan, Ann Arbor.

Carey, I.
 1976 Orang Asli: The Aboriginal Tribes of Peninsular Malaysia. Kuala Lumpur: Oxford University Press.

Carneiro, R. L.
 1960 Slash-and-burn agriculture: A closer look at implications for settlement patterns. In: Men and Cultures, A. F. C. Wallace (ed.). Philadelphia: University of Pennsylvania Press.

 1968 The transition from hunting to horticulture in the Amazon Basin. Vol. III: Anthropology and Archaeology. Proceedings of the Eighth Congress of Anthropological and Ethnological Sciences. Tokyo: Science Council of Japan.

Cashdan, E.
 1979 Trade and Reciprocity among the River Bushmen of Northern Botswana. Ph.D. dissertation. The University of New Mexico.

 1980 Property and social insurance among the //Gana. Second International Conference on Hunting and Gathering Societies. Ste.-Foy, Quebec: Chateau Bonne Entete.

Castillet, E. de R.
 1960 Cagayan Province and Her People. Manila: Community Publishers.

Childe, V. G.
 1951 Man Makes Himself. New York: Mentor Books.

Clark, C.
 1986 Trading Networks of the Northeastern Cagayan Agta. Master's thesis. The University of Hawaii, Honolulu.

Clark, G.
 1951 World Prehistory. Cambridge: Cambridge University Press.

Clarke, W. C.
 1971 Place and People: An Ecology of a New Guinean Community. Canberra: The Australian National University.

Colinvaux, P.
 1978 Why Big Fierce Animals are Rare: An Ecologist's Perspective. Princeton: Princeton University Press.

Collins, P. W.
1965 Functional analyses in man, culture, and animals. In: Man, Culture, and Animals, A. Leeds and A. P. Vayda (eds.). Washington: American Association for the Advancement of Science.

Conklin, H. C.
1957 Hanunoo Agriculture in the Philippines. Rome: Food and Agricultural Organization of the United Nations.

1959a Shifting cultivation and succession to grassland climax. Proceedings of the Ninth Pacific Science congress, Vol. 7. Bangkok.

1959b Population-land balance under systems of tropical forest agriculture. Proceedings of the Ninth Pacific Science Congress, Vol. 7. Bangkok.

1961 The study of shifting cultivation. Current Anthropology, 2:27–61.

1969 An ethnoecological approach to shifting cultivation. In: Environment and Cultural Behavior, A. P. Vayda (ed.). New York: The Natural History Press.

Cooper, H. N.
1940 Andamanese-Semang-Eta cultural relations. Primitive Man, XII(2):29–47.

Coronas, J.
1920 The Climate and Weather of the Philippines, 1903 to 1918. Manila: Bureau of Printing.

Dahmen, F.
1908 The Paliyans: A hill tribe of the Patni Hills, South India. Anthropos, III:19–31.

Damas, D. (ed.)
1969a Contribution to Anthropology: Band Societies. Bulletin No. 228. Ottawa: National Museum of Canada.

1969b Contributions to Anthropology: Ecological Essays. Bulletin No. 230. Ottawa: National Museum of Canada.

Dasmann, R. G.
1974 Ecosystems. Paper presented at the Symposium on the Future of Traditional Primitive Societies. Cambridge, England.

Dasmann, R. F., J. P. Milton and P. H. Freeman
1973 Ecological Principles for Economic Development. London: John Wiley and Sons.

Diong, C. H.
1973 Studies of the Malayan wild pig in Perak and Johore. Malayan Nature Journal, 26:120–51.

Dozier, E. P.
1967 The Kalinga of Northern Luzon, Philippines. New York: Holt, Rinehart and Winston.

Dunn, F. L.
1968 Epidemiological factors: Health and disease in hunter-gatherers. In: Man the Hunter, R. B. Lee and I. DeVore (eds.). Chicago: Aldine Publishing Co.

1975 Rain forest collectors and traders: A study of resource utilization in modern and ancient Malaya. Kuala Lumpur: Malaysian Branch of Royal Asiatic Society.

Durkheim, E.
    1965   The Rules of the Sociological Method. Translated by S. A. Solovay and J. H. Mueller. New York: The Free Press.

Dwyer, P. D.
    1978   Rats, pigs and men: Disturbance and diversity in the New Guinea Highlands. Australian Journal of Ecology, 3:213–32.

Dyson-Hudson, R., and E. A. Smith
    1978   Human territoriality: An ecological reassessment. American Anthropologist, 80(1):21–41.

Eder, J. F.
    1978   The caloric returns to food collecting: Disruption and change among the Batak of the Philippine tropical forest. Human Ecology, 6(1):55–69.

    1987   On the Road to Tribal Extinction: Depopulation, Deculturation and Maladaptation Among the Batak of the Philippines. Berkeley: University of California Press.

    1988   Hunter-gatherer/farmer exchange in the Philippines: Some implications for ethnic identity and adaptive well being. In: Ethnic Diversity and the Control of Natural Resources in Southeast Asia, A. T. Rambo, K. Gillogly and K. L. Hutterer (eds.). Center for South and Southeast Asian Studies. The University of Michigan, Ann Arbor.

Ellen, R. F.
    1979   Introduction: Anthropology, the environment and ecological systems. In: Social and Ecological Systems, P. C. Burnham and R. F. Ellen (eds.). London: Academic Press.

Endicott, K. L.
    1981   The conditions of egalitarian male-female relationships on foraging societies. Canberra Anthropology, 4(2):1–10.

Endicott, Kirk
    1979a   The impact of economic modernization on the Orang Asli (Aborigines) of northern Peninsular Malaysia. In: Issues in Malaysian Development, J. C. Jackson and M. Rudner (eds.). Singapore: Heineman Educational Books.

    1979b   The hunting methods of the Batek Negritos of Malaysia: A problem of alternatives. Canberra Anthropology, 2(2):7–22.

    1979c   Batek Negrito Religion: The Worldview and Rituals of a Hunting and Gathering People of Peninsular Malaysia. Oxford: Oxford University Press.

    1982   The effects of logging on the Batek of Malaysia. In: The Craft of Social Anthropology, A. L. Epstein (ed.), pp. 153–80. New York: Tavistock.

Estioko, A. A., and P. B. Griffin
    1975   The Ebuked Agta of northeastern Luzon. Philippine Quarterly of Culture and Society, 3:237–44.

Estioko-Griffin, A.
    1984   The Ethnography of Southeastern Cagayan Agta Hunting. Master's thesis. The University of the Philippine System, Quezon City.

    1985   Women as hunters: The case of an eastern Cagayan Agta group. In: The Agta of Northeastern Luzon: Recent Studies, P. Bion Griffin and A. Estioko-Griffin (eds.). Cebu City: Univeristy of San Carlos.

Estioko-Griffin, A. and P. B. Griffin
 1981 Woman the hunter: The Agta. In: Woman the Gatherer. F. Dahlberg (ed.). New Haven: Yale University Press.

Evans-Pritchard, E. E.
 1940 The Nuer. Oxford: Clarendon Press.

Evard, A.
 1979 Encounter with a vanishing forest people: The Pugot (Agta) of Isabela. Orientations, 10(11):34–39.

Farnworth, E. G., and F. B. Golley (eds.)
 1974 Fragile Ecosystems. New York: Springer-Verlag.

Fernandez, C. A.
 1972 Blueprints, realities and success in a frontier resettlement community. In: View from the Paddy: Empirical Studies of Philippine Rice Farming and Tenancy, F. Lynch (ed.). Quezon City: Institute of Philippine Culture Publications.

Firth, R.
 1936 We, the Tikopia. London: George, Allen and Unwin.

Flannery, K. V.
 1968 Archeological systems theory and early Meso-America. In: Anthropological Archeology in Americas, B. J. Meggers (ed.). Washington: The Anthropological Society.

 1971 Origins and ecological effects of early domestication in Iran and the Near East. In: Prehistoric Agriculture, S. Struever (ed.). New York: The Natural History Press.

 1972 The cultural evolution of civilizations. American Review of Ecology and Systematics, 3:399–426.

Flores, J. F., and V. F. Balagot
 1969 Climate of the Philippines. In: Climates of Northern and Eastern Asia, H. Arakawa (ed.). World Survey of Climatology, Vol. 8. Amsterdam: Elsevier Publishing Co.

FNRI (Food and Nutrition Research Institute)
 1968 Food Composition Table. Manila: Food and Nutrition Research Institute, National Science Development Board.

Fox, R. B.
 1953 The Pinatubo Negritos: Their useful plants and material culture. Philippine Journal of Science, 81(3-4):173–414.

 1972 The Philippines in prehistoric times. Science Review, 3(9):1–16.

Fox, R. B., and E. Flory
 1974 Map of the Filipino people. (Map.) Manila: National Museum of the Philippines.

Frisch, R.
 1974 A method of prediction of age at menarche from height and weight at ages 9 through 13 years. Pediatrics, 53:384–90.

Gaabucayan, S. P.
 1978 The Pinatubo Negritos of Pampanga-Tarlac Area: A Study of Socio-Cultural Change and Development. Ph.D. dissertation. The University of the Philippine System, Quezon City.

Gardner, P. M.
1972 The Paliyans. In: Hunters and Gatherers Today, M. G. Bicchieri (ed.). New York: Holt, Rinehart and Winston.

Garvan, J. M.
1963 The Negritos of the Philippines, H. Hochegger (ed.). Vienna: Verlag Ferdinand Berger.

Geertz, C.
1963 Agricultural Involution: The Processes of Ecological Change in Indonesia. Berkeley: University of California Press.

Glover, I. C.
1973 Settlements and mobility among the hunter-gatherers of Southeast Asia. In: Man, Settlement and Urbanism, P. Ucko, R. Tringham and G. W. Dimbleby (eds.), pp. 157–64. London: Duckworth.

Goddard, G. W.
1930 The unexplored Philippines from the air. National Geographic, 58:311–43.

Goodenough, W.
1956 Residence rules. Southwestern Journal of Anthropology, 12:22–37.

Gomes, A. G.
1982 Ecological Adaptation and Population Change: Semang Foragers and Temuan Horticulturalists in West Malaysia. East-West Environment and Policy Institute. Research Report No. 12. Honolulu: East-West Center.

1988 The Semai: The making of an ethnic group in Malaysia. In: Ethnic Diversity and the Control of Natural Resources in Southeast Asia, A. T. Rambo, K. Gillogly and K. L. Hutterer (eds.). Center for South and Southeast Asian Studies. The University of Michigan, Ann Arbor.

Goodman, M. J., A. A. Estioko-Griffin and J. S. Grove
1985 Menarche, pregnancy, birth spacing and menopause among the Agta women of northeastern Luzon, Philippines. In: The Agta of Northeastern Luzon: Recent Studies, P. Bion Griffin and A. Estioko-Griffin (eds.). Cebu City: University of San Carlos.

Gould, R. A.
1980 Living Archeology. Cambridge: Cambridge University Press.

Griffin, P. B.
1978 Ethnoarcheology in the Philippines. Archeology, 31(6):34–43.

1985a Population movements and socio-economic change in the Sierra Madre. In: The Agta of Northeastern Luzon: Recent Studies, P. Bion Griffin and A. Estioko-Griffin (eds.). Cebu City: University of San Carlos.

1985b Agta subsistence strategies and the origins of tropical horticulture. In: Recent Advances in Indo-Pacific Prehistory, U.N. Mishra and Peter S. Bellwood (eds.). New Delhi: Oxford and IBH.

1985c Background to the Agta research. In: The Agta of Northeastern Luzon: Recent Studies, P. Bion Griffin and A. Estioko-Griffin (eds.). Cebu City: University of San Carlos.

1986 Forager resource and land use in the humid tropics: The Agta of northeastern Luzon, the Philippines. In: Past and Present in Hunter-Gatherer Studies, Carmel Schrire (ed.), pp. 95–121. Orlando: Academic Press.

Griffin, P. B., and A. Estioko-Griffin
   1978   Ethnoarcheology of Agta hunter-gatherers. Archaeology, 31(6):36–63.

Grime, J. P.
   1979   Plant Strategies and Vegetation Processes. Chichester: John Wiley and Sons.

Gross, D. R., and B. A. Underwood
   1971   Technological change and caloric costs: Sisal agriculture. American Anthropologist, 73(3):725–40.

Guenther, M. G.
   1976   From hunters to squatters: Social and cultural change among the farm San of Ghanzi, Botswana. In: Kalahari Hunter-Gatherers, R. B. Lee and I. DeVore (eds.). Cambridge: Harvard University Press.

Hames, R. B.
   1979   A comparison of the efficiencies of the shotgun and the bow in neotropical forest hunting. Human Ecology, 7(3):219–52.

Hanks, L.
   1972   Rice and Man: Agricultural Ecology of Southeast Asia. Chicago: Aldine Publishing Co.

Harako, R.
   1976   The Mbuti as hunters: A study of ecological anthropology of the Mbuti Pygmies. Kyoto University African Studies, X:37–100.

Hardesty, D. L.
   1977   Ecological Anthropology. New York: John Wiley and Sons.

Harpending, H.
   1976   Regional variation in !Kung populations. In: Kalahari Hunter-Gatherers, R. B. Lee and I. DeVore (eds.). Cambridge: Harvard University Press.

Harris, D. R.
   1972   Swidden systems and settlement. In: Man, Settlement and Urbanism, P. J. Ucko, R. Tringham and G. W. Dimbleby (eds.). London: Duckworth.

Harris, M.
   1977   Cannibals and Kings: The Origins of Culture. New York: Random House.

   1978   Cows, Pigs, Wars and Witches. New York: Vintage Books.

Harrison, G. A., J. S. Weiner, J. M. Tanner and N. A. Barnicott
   1977   Human Biology. Oxford: Oxford University Press.

Harrison, T.
   1949   Notes on some nomadic Punans. Sarawak Museum Journal, 5(1):130–46.

Hart, C. M. W., and A. R. Pilling
   1960   The Tiwi of North Australia. New York: Holt, Rinehart and Winston.

Hayden, B.
   1981   Research and development in the Stone Age: Technological transitions among hunter-gatherers. Current Anthropology, 22(5):519–48.

Hazewinkle, J. C.
1935 De Koeboe's van Zuid-Sumatra. Natuurkundig Tijdschrift voor Nederlandsch Indie, XCV:110–17.

Headland, T. N.
1975 Report of eastern Luzon language survey. Philippine Journal of Linguistics, 6:47–54.

1978 Cultural ecology, ethnicity, and the Negritos of northeastern Luzon: A review article. Asian Perspectives, XXI(I):127–39.

1981 Taxonomic Disagreement in a Culturally Salient Domain: Botany versus Utility in a Philippine Negrito Taxonomic System. Master's thesis. The University of Hawaii, Honolulu.

1986 Why Foragers Do Not Become Farmers: A Historical Study of a Changing Ecosystem and its Effect on a Negrito Hunter-Gatherer Group in the Philippines. Ph.D. dissertation. The University of Hawaii, Honolulu. (Forthcoming publication of the Museum of Anthropology, University of Michigan).

1987a Kinship and social behavior among Agta Negrito hunter-gatherers. Ethnology, 26(4):261–80.

1987b The wild yam question: How well could independent hunter-gatherers live in a tropical rain forest ecosystem. Human Ecology, 15(4):463–91.

Headland, T. N., and J. D. Headland
1974 A Dumagat (Casiguran)-English Dictionary. Pacific Linguistics, C (28). Canberra: The Australian National University.

1984 Casiguran Dumagat kinship terminology. In: A Sampling of Philippine Kinship Patterns, Richard E. Elkins and Gail R. Hendrickson (eds.), pp. 69–73. Manila: Summer Institute of Linguistics.

Headland, T. N., and L. A. Reid
1989 Hunter-gatherers and their neighbors from prehistory to the present. Current Anthropology, 30(1):43–66.

Heine-Geldern, R.
1957 Introduction: Urgent anthropological research. Disappearing Cultures: International Social Science Bulletin, IX(3):277–351.

Helm, J.
1962 The ecological approach in anthropology. The American Journal of Sociology, 67:630–39.

Hernandez, P. P.
1954 Rainfall Types Based on Ratios of Dry Months to Wet Months. Manila: Weather Bureau.

Hiatt, L. R.
1968 Ownership and use of land among the Australian aborigines. In: Man the Hunter, R. B. Lee and I. DeVore (eds.). Chicago: Aldine Publishing Co.

Hoffman, Carl L.
1984 Punan foragers in the trading networks of Southeast Asia. In: Past and Present in Hunter-Gatherer Studies, Carmel Schrire (ed.). Orlando: Academic Press.

1986 The Punan: Hunters and gatherers of Borneo. Ph.D. disssertation. The University of Michigan.

Howell, N.
1976 The population of the Dobe area !Kung. In: Kalahari Hunter-Gatherers, R. B. Lee and I. DeVore (eds.). Cambridge: Harvard University Press.

1979 Demography of the Dobe !Kung. New York: Academic Press.

1980 Demographic behavior of hunter-gatherers: Evidence for density dependent population control. In: Demographic Behavior, T. K. Burch (ed.). Washington, D.C.: American Association for the Advancement of Science.

Hutterer, K. L.
1976 An evolutionary approach to the Southeast Asian cultural sequence. Current Anthropology, 17(2):221-42.

1977 Prehistoric trade and the evolution of Philippine societies: A reconsideration. In: Economic Exchange and Social Interaction in Southeast Asia, K. L. Hutterer (ed.). Center for South and Southeast Asian Studies. The University of Michigan, Ann Arbor.

1979 Review of J. T. Peterson's *The Ecology of Social Boundaries*. Journal of Asian Studies, XXXVIII(4):847-49.

1982 Interaction between tropical ecosystems and human foragers: Some general considerations. Working Paper. East-West Environment and Policy Institute. Honolulu: East-West Center.

1983 The natural and cultural history of Southeast Asian agriculture: Ecological and evolutionary considerations. Anthropos, 78:169-212.

1984 Ecology and evolution of agriculture in Southeast Asia. In: An Introduction to Human Ecology Research on Agricultural Systems in Southeast Asia, A. T. Rambo and P. E. Sajise (eds.). Los Baños: University of the Philippines.

1985 People and nature in the tropics: Remarks concerning ecological relationships. In: Cultural Values and Human Ecology in Southeast Asia, K. L. Hutterer, A. T. Rambo and G. Lovelace (eds.). Center for South and Southeast Asian Studies, University of Michigan, Ann Arbor.

Ingold, T.
1980 The principle of individual autonomy, and the collective appropriation of nature. Second International Conference on Hunting and Gathering Societies. Ste.-Foy, Quebec: Chateau Bonne Entete.

Jochim, M. A.
1976 Hunter-Gatherer Subsistence and Settlement: A Predictive Model. New York: Academic Press.

1979 Breaking down the system: Recent ecological approaches in archeology. In: Advances in Archeological Method and Theory, M. Schiffer (ed.). New York: Academic Press.

Jurika, S.
1962 The Political Geography of the Philippines. Ann Arbor: University Microfilms International.

Kagaoa, M. P.
    1968   Report on San Mariano (Isabela) minorities to the Chairman, Commission on National Integration. Typescript, 3 pages. May 12.

Kedit, P. M.
    1982   An ecological survey of the Penan. The Sarawak Museum Journal, 30(5):225–79.

Keesing, F. M.
    1962   The Ethnohistory of Northern Luzon. Stanford: Stanford University Press.

Keesing, R. M.
    1975   Kin Groups and Social Structure. New York: Holt, Rinehart and Winston.

Kerkvilet, B. J.
    1979   The Huk Rebellion: A Study of Peasant Revolt in the Phillipines. Quezon City: New Day Publishers.

King, F. B., and R. W. Graham
    1981   Effects of ecological and paleoecological patterns on subsistence and paleoenvironment recontructions. American Antiquity, 46(1):128–42.

King, V. T.
    1976   Conceptual and analytical problems in the study of the kindred. In: The Societies of Borneo, G. N. Appell (ed.). Washington: American Anthropological Association.

Knoebel, L. K.
    1976   Energy metabolism. In: Physiology, E. E. Selkurt (ed.). Boston: Little, Brown and Co.

Kroeber, A. L.
    1928   Peoples of the Philippines. New York: American Museum of Natural History.

Kunstadter, P., E. C. Chapman and S. Sabhasri (eds.)
    1978   Farmers in the Forest: Economic Development and Marginal Agriculture in Northern Thailand. Honolulu: University of Hawaii Press.

Larkin, J. A.
    1972   The Pampangans: Colonial Society in a Philippine Province. Berkeley: University of California Press.

Leach, E. R.
    1954   Political Systems of Highland Burma: A Study of Kachin Social Structure. London: G. Bell and Sons.

Lebar, F.
    1975   Negritos. In: Ethnic Groups of Insular Southeast Asia, Vol. 2, Frank Lebar (ed.). New Haven: Human Relations Area Files.

Lee, R. B.
    1968   What hunters do for a living or How to make out on scarce resources. In: Man the Hunter, R. B. Lee and I. DeVore (eds.). Chicago: Aldine Publishing Co.

    1969   !Kung Bushman subsistence: An input-output analysis. In: Environment and Cultural Behavior, A. P. Vayda (ed.). New York: The Natural History Press.

    1972a !Kung spatial organization : An ecological and historical perspective. Human Ecology, 1:125–47.

1972b The intensification of social life among the !Kung Bushmen. In: Population Growth: Anthropological Implications, B. Spooner (ed.). Cambridge: The MIT Press.

1978 Issues in the study of hunter-gatherers, 1968-1978. Discussion paper for the Conference on International Research on Hunters and Gatherers, Paris (June).

1979 The !Kung San: Men, Women and Work in a Foraging Society. Cambridge: Cambridge University Press.

Lee, R. B., and I. DeVore (eds.)
1968 Man the Hunter. Chicago: Aldine Publishing Co.

Levine, T. Y.
1981 Forest Peoples of the Philippines: The Batak and Palawano. University of California at Los Angeles, Museum of Cultural History, Pamphlet Series 15.

Lewis, H. T.
1971 Ilocano Rice Farmers: Comparative Study of Two Philippine Barrios. Honolulu: University of Hawaii Press.

Lieban, R. W.
1967 Cebuano Sorcery: Malign Magic in the Philippines. Berkeley: University of California Press.

MacCormack, C.
1978 The cultural ecology of production: Sherbro coast and hinterland, Sierra Leone. In: Social Organization and Settlement, D. R. Green, C. C. Haselgrove and M. J. T. Spriggs (eds.). Oxford: British Archeological Reports.

Maceda, M. N.
1964 The Culture of the Mamanua (Northeast Mindanao) as Compared With That of the Other Negritos of Southeast Asia. Manila: Catholic Trade School.

1974 A survey of landed property concepts and practices among the marginal agriculturalists of the Philippines. Philippine Quarterly of Culture and Society, 2:5–21.

Malinowski, B.
1922 Argonauts of the Western Pacific. London: Routledge and Kegan Paul.

Man, E. H.
1883 On the Aboriginal Inhabitats of the Andaman Islands. London: Trubner.

Margalef, R.
1968 Perspectives in Ecological Theory. Chicago: University of Chicago Press.

Marten, G.
1984 The tropical rain forest as an ecosystem. In: An Introduction to Human Ecology Research on Agricultural Systems in Southeast Asia, A. T. Rambo and P. E. Sajise (eds.). Los Baños: University of the Philippines.

Maruyama, A.
1963 The second cybernetics: Deviation-amplifying mutual causal processes. American Scientist, 51:164–79, 250–56.

May, R. M.
1973 Stability and Complexity in Model Ecosystems. Princeton: Princeton University Press.

Maynard, L. A., and J. K. Loosli
  1969 Animal Nutrition. New York: McGraw Hill.

McArthur, M.
  1974 Pigs for the ancestors: A review article. Oceania, XLV(2):87–132.

McLennan, M. S.
  1980 The Central Luzon Plain: Land and Society on the Inland Frontier. Quezon City: Alemar-Phoenix Publishers.

MDS (Municipality Development Survey)
  1979 Socioeconomic Profile: San Mariano, Isabela. San Mariano: Mayor's Office.

Mech, L. D.
  1979 Why some deer are safe from wolves. Natural History, 88(1):70–77.

Merrill, E. D.
  1945 Plant Life of the Pacific World. New York: The Macmillan Company.

  1967 An Enumeration of Philippine Flowering Plants. Vol. 4. Amsterdam: A. Ascher and Co.

Milton, K.
  1981 Distribution patterns of tropical plant foods as an evolutionary stimulus to primate development. American Anthropologist, 83(3):534–48.

Mitchell, J. C.
  1949 An estimate of fertility in some Yao hamlets in Liwonde District of southern Nyasaland. Africa, 19(4):293-308.

Mitchell, W. E.
  1963 Theoretical problems in the concept of kindred. American Anthropologist, 65:343–54.

Morris, B.
  1977 Tappers, trappers and the Hill Pandaran, South India. Anthropos, 72:225–41.

Mudar, K. M.
  1985 Bearded pigs and beardless men: Predator-prey relationships between pigs and Agta in northeastern Luzon, Philippines. In: The Agta of Northeastern Luzon: Recent Studies, P. Bion Griffin and A. Estioko-Griffin (eds.). Cebu City: University of San Carlos.

Murdock, G. P.
  1960 Cognatic forms of social organizations. In: Social Structure in Southeast Asia, G. P. Murdock (ed.). Chicago: Quadrangle Books.

  1967 Ethnographic atlas: A summary. Ethnology, 6:109–236.

  1968 The current status of the world's hunting and gathering peoples. In: Man the Hunter, R. B. Lee and I. DeVore (eds.). Chicago: Aldine Publishing Co.

  1969 Correlations of exploitative and settlement patterns. In: Contributions to Anthropology: Ecological Essays, D. Damas (ed.). Ottawa: National Museum of Canada.

Murphy, R. F., and J. H. Steward
  1956 Tappers and trappers: Parallel process in acculturation. Economic Development and Social Change, 4:335–53.

References Cited

Myers, N.
1980 Conversion of Tropical Moist Forests. Washington, D.C.: National Academy of Sciences.

Nag, M.
1980 How modernization can also increase fertility. Current Anthropology, 21(5):571–87.

Nance, J.
1981 Discovery of the Tasaday: A Photo Novel: The Stone Age Meets the Space Age in the Philippine Rain Forest. Manila: Vera-Reyes.

Needham, R.
1954 A note on some nomadic Punan. Indonesie, VII:520–23.

Neel, J. V., and N. A. Chagnon
1968 The demography of primitive, relatively unaccultured American Indians. Proceedings of the National Academy of Sciences, 59:680–89.

Newton, P.
1920 Observations on the Negritos of the Philippines. American Journal of Physical Anthropology, 3:1–24.

Nickell, T. L.
1985 A partial stratificational analysis of eastern Cagayan Agta Language. In: The Agta of Northeastern Luzon: Recent Studies, P. Bion Griffin and A. Estioko-Griffin (eds.). Cebu City: University of San Carlos.

Nicolaisen, J.
1974 The Negritos of Casiguran Bay: Problems of affluency, territoriality and human aggres-
–75   siveness in hunting societies of Southeast Asia. Folk: Dansk Ethnografisk Tidsskrift, 16–17:401–34.

Nietschmann, B.
1973 Between Land and Water: The Subsistence Ecology of the Miskito Indians, Eastern Nicaragua. New York: Seminar Press.

Nimmo, H. A.
1969 The Structure of Bajau Society. Ph.D. dissertation. The University of Hawaii, Honolulu.

NWRC (National Water Resource Council)
1976 Principal River Basins of the Philippines. Report No. 4. Manila: National Water Resource Council.

Odum, E. P.
1959 Fundamentals of Ecology. Philadelphia: Saunders.

1975 Ecology. New York: Holt, Rinehart and Winston.

Odum, H. T.
1971 Environment, Power, and Society. New York: John Wiley and Sons.

Ogawa, H.
1985 Piñobranca Negrito (Peñablanca Negrito). (In Japanese.) Ethnos, 27:13–20, 55–73

Olsen, R. A., R. B. Clark and J. H. Bennett
1918 The enhancement of soil fertility by plant roots. American Scientist, 69(4):378–84.

Omoto, K.
1981 The genetic origins of the Philippine Negritos. Current Anthropology, 22(4):421–22.

1985 The Negritos: Genetic origins and microevolution. In: Out of Asia: Peopling the Americas and the Pacific, Robert Kirk and Emoke Szathmary (eds.), pp. 123–31. Canberra: The Journal of Pacific History.

Parry, W. J.
1982 Observations on the arrow technology of the Negritos of the northern Negros. In: Houses Built on Scattered Poles: Prehistory and Ecology in Negros Oriental, Philippines, Karl L. Hutterer and W. K. Macdonald (eds.), pp. 107–16. Cebu City: University of San Carlos.

Pascacio, F.M., W. B. Bias, V. Manipol, and P. C. Campos
1974 Genetic marker systems in Philippine Negritos. Birth Defects: Original Article Series, 10(10):220–25.

PDA (Provincial Development Administration)
1978 Provincial Profile: Isabela. Ilagan: Provincial Development Administration.

Pelzer, K. J.
1945 Pioneer Settlement in the Asiatic Tropics. New York: Institute of Pacific Relations.

Pennoyer, F. D.
1975 Taubuid Plants and Ritual Complexes. Ph.D. dissertation. Washington State University.

Peterson, J. T.
1976 Folk traditions and interethnic relations in northeastern Luzon, Philippines. In: Directions in Pacific Traditional Literature, A. L. Kaeppler and H. A. Nimmo (eds.). Honolulu: Bishop Museum Press.

1977a Ecotones and exhange in northern Luzon. In: Economic Exchange and Social Interaction in Southeast Asia, K. L. Hutterer (ed.). Center for South and Southeast Asian Studies. The University of Michigan, Ann Arbor.

1977b The merits of margins. In: Cultural-Ecological Perspectives on Southeast Asia, W. Wood (ed.). Athens: Ohio University Center for International Studies.

1978a The Ecology of Social Boundaries: Agta Foragers of the Philippines. Urbana: University of Illinois Press.

1978b Hunter-gatherer/farmer exchange. American Anthropologist, 80(2):335–51.

1981 Game, farming, and interethnic relations in northeastern Luzon, Philippines. Human Ecology, 9(1):1–22.

1982 The effect of farming expansion on hunting. Philippine Sociological Review, 30:33–50.

1984 Cash, consumerism, and savings: Economic change Among the Agta foragers of Luzon, Philippines. Research in Economic Anthropology, 6:53–73.

1985 Hunter mobility, family organization and change. In: Circulation in Third World Countries, R. Munsell Prothero and Murry Chapman (eds.), pp. 124–44. London: Routledge and Kegan Paul.

Peterson, J. T., and W. Peterson
  1977 Implications of contemporary and prehistoric exchange systems. In: Sunda and Sahul: Prehistoric Studies in Southeast Asia, Melanesia and Australia, J. Allen, J. Golson and R. Jones (eds.). New York: Academic Press.

Peterson, N.
  1979 Territorial adaptations among desert hunter-gatherers: The !Kung and Australians compared. In: Social and Ecological Systems, P. C. Burnham and R. F. Ellen (eds.). London: Academic Press.

Peterson, W.
  1974 Summary report of two archeological sites from north-eastern Luzon. Archeology and Physical Anthropology in Oceania, 9:26–35.

  1981 Recent adaptive shifts among Palanan hunters of the Philippines. Man, 16:43–61.

Philippine Commission
  1908 Eighth Annual Report of the Philippine Commission, 1907. Washington: Government Printing Office.

Philippine Yearbook
  1983 Philippine Yearbook, 1983. Manila: National Census and Statistics Office.

Pianka, E. R.
  1978 Evolutionary Ecology. New York: Harper and Row Publishers.

Pike, K. L.
  1966 Etic and emic standpoints for the desciption of behavior. In: Communication and Culture, A. G. Smith (ed.). New York: Holt, Rinehart and Winston.

  1967 Language in Relation to a Unified Theory of the Structure and Human Behavior. The Hague: The Mouton Publishers.

Pili, M. U.
  1979 The Agta of Mount Asog, City of Iriga. Ph.D. dissertation. University of Saint Anthony, Iriga.

Radcliffe-Brown, A. R.
  1931 Social Organization of Australian Tribes. Oceania Monographs No. 1.

  1932 The Andaman Islanders. Glencoe: The Free Press.

  1952 Structure and Function in Primitive Society. Glencoe: The Free Press.

Rahmann, R.
  1963 The Negritos of the Philippines and the early Spanish missionaries. Studia Instituti Anthropos, 18:137–57.

  1975 The Philippine Negritos in the context of research on food gatherers during this century. Philippine Quarterly of Culture and Society, 3:204–36.

  1985 The nocturnal prayer ceremonies of the Negritos of the Philippines. Philippine Quarterly of Culture and Society, 13(6):262–81.

Rai, N. K.
  1981 Under the shadow of soft gold: The impact of the logging industry on a hunter-gatherer society. Impulse, 8(1):48–50.

1982 From Forest to Field: A Study of Philippine Negrito Foragers in Transition. Ph.D. dissertation. The University of Hawaii, Honolulu.

1983 Concept of native environment and its implications to resource use: A case of the Agta foragers of the Philippines. Paper read at the Proceedings of the Third International Conference on Hunter-Gatherers, Bad Homburg, June 13–16.

1985 Ecology in ideology: An example from the Agta foragers. In: The Agta of Northeastern Luzon: Recent Studies, P. Bion Griffin and A. Estioko-Griffin (eds.). Cebu City: University of San Carlos.

Rambo, A. T.
1979 Primitive man's impact on genetic resources of the Malaysian tropical rain forest. Malaysian Applied Biology, 8(1):59–65.

1982 Orang Asli adaptive strategies: Implications for Malaysian natural resource development planning. In: Too Rapid Rural Development: Perceptions and Perspectives from Southeast Asia, Colin MacAndrews and Chia Lin Sien (eds.), pp. 251–99. Athens: Ohio University Press.

1984 Orang Asli interactions with the Malaysian tropical rain forest ecosystem. In: An Introduction to Human Ecology Research on Agricultural Systems in Southeast Asia, A. T. Rambo and P. E. Sajise (eds.), pp. 237–53. Los Baños: University of the Philippines.

1988 Why are the Semang? Ecology and ethnogenesis of aboriginal groups in Peninsular Malaysia. In: Ethnic Diversity and the Control of Natural Resources in Southeast Asia, A. T. Rambo, R. Gillogly and K. L. Hutterer (eds.). Center for South and Southeast Asian Studies. The University of Michigan, Ann Arbor.

Rappaport, Roy A.
1968 Pigs for the ancestors: Rituals in the ecology of a New Guinea People. New Haven: Yale University Press.

1969a Some suggestions concerning concept and method in ecological anthropology. In: Contributions to Anthropology: Ecological Essays, D. Damas (ed.). Ottawa: National Museum of Canada.

1969b Ritual regulation of environmental relations among a New Guinea people. In: Environment and Cultural Behavior, A. P. Vayda (ed.). New York: The Natural History Press.

1979 Ecology, Meaning and Religion. Richmond: North Atlantic Books.

Raven, P. H.
1981 Tropical Rain Forest: A Global Responsibility. Natural History, 90(2):28–32.

Reed, W. A.
1904 Negritos of Zambales, Philippine Islands. Vol. 2. Ethnological Survey Publications. Manila: Bureau of Printing.

Reid, L. A. (ed.)
1971 Philippine Minor Languages: Word Lists and Phonologies. Honolulu: University of Hawaii Press.

Reynolds, H.
1976 The development project of the mountain Negritos of Northern Negros, Philippines. Siliman Journal 23:182–202.

Rhoades, R. E.
1978 Archeological use and abuse of ecological concepts and studies: The ecotone example. American Antiquity, 43(4):608–14.

Rice, D., and R. Tima
1973 A Pattern for Development. Quezon City: Christian Institute for Ethnic Studies in Asia.

Richards, P. W.
1979 The Tropical Rain Forest. London: Cambridge University Press.

Rosaldo, R.
1980 Ilongot Headhunting, 1883–1974: A Study in History and Society. Stanford: Stanford University Press.

1983 Utter savages of scientific value. In: Politics and History in Band Societies, Eleanor Leacock and Richard B. Lee (eds.), pp. 309–26. Cambridge: Cambridge University Press.

Sahlins, M. D.
1965 On the sociology of primitive exchange. In: The Relevance of Models of Social Anthropology. ASA Monograph. London: Tavistock.

Salisbury, R. F.
1962 From Stone to Steel: Economic Consequences of a Technological Change in New Guinea. London: Cambridge University Press.

Sather, C. A.
1976 Kinship and contiguity: Variation in social alignments among the Semporna Bajau Laut. In: The Societies of Borneo, G. N. Appell (ed.). Washington: American Anthropological Association.

Schebesta, P.
1927 Among the Forest Dwarfs of Malaya (translated by A. Chambers). London: Hutchinson and Co.

1952 Die Negrito Asiens. Vienna-Molding: St. Gabriel Verlag.
–57

Schlegel, S. A.
1979 Tiruray Subsistence: From Shifting Cultivation to Plow Agriculture. Quezon City: Ateneo de Manila University Press.

Schottelius, B. A., and D. D. Schottelius
1978 Physiology. St. Louis: The C. V. Mosby Company.

Schusky, E. L.
1972 Manual for Kinship Analysis. New York: Holt, Rinehart and Winston.

Scott, W. H.
1979 Semper's "Kalingas": 120 years later. Philippine Sociological Review, 27(20):91–101.

1984 Prehispanic Source Materials for the Study of Philippine History. Quezon City: New Day Publishers.

Segovia, L.
1969 The Full Story of Aguinaldo's Capture (translated by F. de Thoma). Manila: MCS Enterprises.

Semper, C.
1861 Reise durch die Nordöstlichen Provinzen der Insel Luzon. Zeitschrift fur Allgemeine Erdkunde, 10:249-66.

1869 Die Philippinen und ihre Bowehner: Sechs Skizzon. Wurzburg: A. Stuber's Buchhandlung.

Serevo, T. S.
1949 Some observations on the effects of different methods of logging on residual stand and on natural reproduction. Philippine Journal of Forestry, 6(4):363-81.

Service, E. R.
1966 The Hunters. Englewood Cliffs: Prentice Hall.

Shafer, R.
1940 Nahili: A linguistic study in paleoethnography. Harvard Journal of Asiatic Studies, V:346-71.

Shimizu, H.
1981 Marriage and bridewealth among southwestern Mt. Pinatubo Negritos, Zambales, in relation to the composition of the extended family. Japanese Journal of Ethnology, 46(1):35-54.

Shuttles, W.
1968 Coping with abundance: Subsistence on the Northwest Coast. In: Man the Hunter, R. B. Lee and I. DeVore (eds.). Chicago: Aldine Publishing Co.

Silberbauer, G. B.
1972 The G/wi Bushmen. In: Hunters and Gatherers Today, M. G. Bicchieri (ed.). New York: Holt, Rinehart and Winston.

1981 Hunter and Habitat in the Central Kalahari Desert. Cambridge: Cambridge University Press.

Simangan, M.
1956 The Negritos of Palanan, Isabela: Their Life and Culture. Master's thesis. National University, Manila.

Simon, S.
1982 The Community Life of the Dumagats of Palanan, Isabela: Its Implications to Development. Ph.D. dissertation. St. Paul University, Tuguegurao, Cagayan.

Sinha, D. P.
1972 The Birhors. In: Hunters and Gatherers Today, M. G. Bicchieri (ed.). New York: Holt, Rinehart, and Winston.

Slayter, R. O.
1977 Dynamic Changes in Terrestrial Ecosystems. Paris: UNESCO.

Solheim, W. G.
1981 Philippine prehistory. In: The People and the Art of the Philippines, G. Casal, et al. (eds.). The University of California, Los Angeles.

Spencer, J. E.
1966 Shifting Cultivation in Southeast Asia. Berkeley: University of California Press.

Speth, J. D.
n.d.a   Seasonality, resource stress, and food sharing in so-called "egalitarian" foraging societies. (Manuscript.)

n.d.b   Some unexplored aspects of mutualistic plains/pueblo food exchange. (Manuscript.)

n.d.c   Hunting vs. scavenging: The overemphasis on protein. (Manuscript.)

Speth, J. D. and K. A. Spielmann
1983   Energy source, protein metabolism and hunter-gatherer subsistence strategies. Journal of Anthropological Archeology, 2:1–31.

Spottswood, C. L.
1961   Beyond Cotabato. Westwood, N.J.: Fleming H. Revell.

Steward, J. H.
1936   The economic and social basis of primitive bands. In: Essays in Anthropology Presented to A. K. Kroeber. Berkeley: University of California Press.

1938   Basin Plateau Aboriginal Sociopolitical Groups. Washington: Smithsonian Institution.

1955   Theory of Culture Change: The Methodology of Multilinear Evolution. Urbana: University of Illinois Press.

Tagudar, E. T., and P. O. Quintana
1957   Tractor selective logging techniques practiced by the Nasipit Lumber Company. The Philippine Journal of Forestry, 13(3–4):221–32.

Tharp, J.
1974   The northern Cordilleran sub-group of Philippine languages. Working Paper in Linguistics, 6(6):53-114.

Thomas, R. B., B. Winterhalder and S. D. McRae
1979   An anthropological approach to human ecology and adaptive dynamics. Yearbook of Physical Anthropology, 22:1–46.

Townsend, N.
1978   Biased symbiosis on the Tana River. In: The Nomadic Alternative, W. Weissler (ed.). Paris: The Mouton Publishers.

Turnbull, C. M.
1962   The Forest People: A Study of the Pygmies of Congo. New York: Simon and Schuster.

1965   Wayward Servants: The Two Worlds of the African Pygmies. Garden City: The Natural History Press.

1968   The importance of flux in two hunting societies. In: Man the Hunter, R. B. Lee and I. DeVore (eds.). Chicago: Aldine Publishing Co.

1972   The Mountain People. New York: Simon and Schuster.

Turnbull, W.
1929   The "Dumagats" of north-east Luzon. Philippine Magazine, 26(3):131–33, 175–78, 26(4):208–9, 237–40.

1930   Bringing a wild tribe under government control. Philippine Magazine, 26(12):782–98, 27(1):21–120.

Vanoverbergh, M.
  1937   Some Undescribed Languages of Luzon. Nijmegen: Dekker and Van.

  1937   Negritos of eastern Luzon. Anthropos, 32:905–28, 33:119–64.
  –38

Vayda, A. P., and R. A. Rappaport
  1968   Ecology: Cultural and non-cultural. In: Introduction to Cultural Anthropology, J. Clifton (ed.). Boston: Houghton Mifflin Co.

Vayda, A. P., and B. McCay
  1975   New directions in ecology and ecological anthropology. Annual Review of Anthropology, 4:293–306.

Vickers, W. T.
  1988   Game depletion hypothesis of Amazonian adaptation: Data from a native community. Science, 239:1521–22.

von Bertalanffy, L.
  1968   General systems theory: A critical review. In: Modern Systems Research for the Behavioral Scientist, W. Buckley (ed.). Chicago: Aldine Publishing Co.

Wallace, B. J.
  1970a Hill and Valley Farmers: Socioeconomic Change Among a Philippine People. Cambridge: Schenkman Publishing Co.

  1970b Agricultural technology of the Pagan Gaddang. In: Cultures of the Pacific, T. G. Harding and B. J. Wallace (eds.). New York: The Free Press.

Warren, C. P.
  1964   The Batak of Palawan: A Culture in Transition. Philippine Studies Program, University of Chicago.

Wastl, J.
  1957   Beitrag zur anthropologie der Negrito von Ost-Luzon. Anthropos, 52:769–812.

Watanabe, H.
  1968   Subsistence and ecology of northern food gatherers with special reference to the Ainu. In: Man the Hunter, R. B. Lee and I. DeVore (eds.). Chicago: Aldine.

  1972   The Ainu. In: Hunters and Gatherers Today, M. G. Bicchieri (ed.). New York: Holt, Rinehart, and Winston.

Weissner, P. W.
  1977   Hxaro: A Regional System of Reciprocity for Reducing Risk Among the !Kung San. Ann Arbor: University Microfilms International.

Wernsted, F. L., and J. E. Spencer
  1967   The Philippine Island World: A Physical, Cultural and Regional Geography. Berkeley: University of California Press.

Whitford, H. N.
  1960   The vegetation of Lamao Forest Reserve, Philippines. Philippine Journal of Science, 1(4):373–429, (6):637–81.

  1911   The Forests of the Philippines. Bureau of Forestry Bulletin No. 10. Manila: Bureau of Printing.

References Cited

Williams, B. J.
 1968 The Birhor of India and some comments on band organization. In: Man the Hunter, R. B. Lee and I. DeVore (eds.). Chicago: Aldine Publishing Co.

Woodburn, J.
 1968a An introduction to Hadza ecology. In: Man the Hunter, R. B. Lee and I. DeVore (eds.). Chicago: Aldine Publishing Co.

 1968b Stability and flexibility in Hadza residential groupings. In: Man the Hunter, R. B. Lee and I. DeVore (eds.). Chicago: Aldine Publishing Co.

 1980 An approach to the ethnography of property and sharing. Second International Conference on Hunting and Gathering Societies. Ste-Foy, Quebec: Chataeu Bonne Entete.

Worcester, D.
 1912 Headhunters of northern Luzon. National Geographic, 23:833–930.

 1913 Slavery and Peonage in the Philippine Islands. Manila: Bureau of Printing.

 1955 Domestic economy of the Domagats. Pontifica Accademia delle Scienze (Rome) Acta. Vol. 18.

Yellen, J., and H. Harpending
 1972 Hunter-gatherer populations and archeological inference. World Archeology, 4:244–53.

Yengoyan, A. A.
 1971 The Philippines: The effects of cash cropping on Mandaya land tenure. In: Land Tenure in the Pacific, R. Crocombe (ed.). Melbourne: Oxford University Press.

Zipagang, A.
 1970 A Survey of Dumagat Culture in Palanan, Isabela. Master's thesis. The University of Santo Tomas, Manila.

PLATES

PLATE 1. Agta by the Diwago River. [San Mariano, Isabela, 1979: Photo by Bion Griffin]

PLATE 2. Southeastern Cagayan Agta in fishing camp on the Malibu River. [Peñablanca Municipality, 1982: Photo by Agnes Estioko-Griffin]

PLATE 3. Another view of fishing camp on the Malibu River [See Plate 2: Photo by Agnes Estioko-Griffin]

PLATE 4. Agta dry season houses. [Maconacon Municipality, Isabela, 1981: Photo by Bion Griffin]

PLATE 5. Agta men spearfishing in the Malibu River. [Peñablanca Municipality, 1980: Photo by author]

PLATE 6. *Caryota* palm processing. [Dipagsénghan, Palanan Municipality, 1975: Photo by Bion Griffin]

PLATE 7. Agta man and children. [Dianggu River, Peñablanca Municipality, 1982; Photo by Agnes Estioko-Griffin]

PLATE 8. Agta family leaving on a hunting and fishing trip. [Nanadukan, Peñablanca Municipality, 1980: Photo by Agnes Estioko-Griffin]

PLATE 9. A young, unmarried Agta man. [Disabungan, San Mariano Municipality, 1979: Photo by author]

PLATE 10. A young, unmarried Agta woman. [Diwago River, San Mariano Municipality, 1979: Photo by author]

APPENDIX 1
Population Distribution, by Municipality, of the Agta Negritos of Isabela (1979-1980)[a]

		Population Distribution				Average Distance from Nearest[b]				% of Families	
Watershed	Municipality	River Valleys	Camps		Population	Agta Camp	Agri. Barrio		Logging Camp	Swiddening	Not Swiddening
Valley	Jones	0.5	1		30	35.0	16.0		?[c]	?	?
	San Mariano	4.5	19		332	3.6	8.8		5.5	76.4	23.6
	Ilagan	2	5		68	2.8	28.2		11.4	90.0	10.0
	Tumawini	1	1		11	18.0	14.0		14.0	100.0	0.0
	SUBTOTAL	8	26		441	5.2	13.0		7.0	80.0	20.0[d]
Coastal	Dinapique	2	2		45	17.0	2.0		?	?	?
	Palanan	6	21		669[d]	4.9	3.0		?	97.6	2.4
	Divilacan	13	16		230	3.0	2.4		3.0	100.0	0.0
	Maconacon	13	15		259	3.7	6.6		11.6	86.7	13.3
	SUBTOTAL	34	54		1,203	4.2	3.8		10.3	95.7	4.3
TOTAL	8	42	80		1,644	4.5	6.8		8.3	91.8	8.2

[a]The census was conducted in 1979-1980 by the author.
[b]In kilometers, measured by pedometer strapped to field worker's belt.
[c]Unknown or not calculated.
[d]Provided by Hilarion Gonzales, Palanan.

APPENDIX 2
Population Distribution, by Socioresidential Unit, of the Agta Negritos of Isabela

Linguistic Group	Watershed Group	River Valley Groups	Bands	Population			No. of Families	% of Household Type	
				Male	Female	Total		Nuclear	Other
Ilagin-Dikaméy	valley	1.5	8	69	80	149	38	57.9	42.1
	SUBTOTAL	1.5	8	69	80	149	38	57.9	42.1
Disabungan-	valley	1.5	6	67	71	138	29	62.1	37.9
Dipagsénghan	coastal	3.5	7	118	121	239	59	61.0	39.0
	SUBTOTAL	5	13	185	192	377	88	61.4	38.6
Palanan-Divilacan	valley	2	6	34	41	75	16	50.0	50.0
	coastal	18.5	33	385	396	781	193	62.2	37.8
	SUBTOTAL	20.5	39	419	437	856	209	61.2	38.8
Maconacon-Abuan	valley	3	6	37	42	79	23	52.2	47.8
	coastal	12	14	96	87	183	42	40.5	59.5
	SUBTOTAL	15	20	133	129	262	65	44.6	55.4
TOTAL	7	42	80	806	838	1,644	400	58.3	41.7

APPENDIX 3
Shared Basic Vocabulary Among Languages Spoken in Northeastern Luzon, based on Reid's (1971) Word List

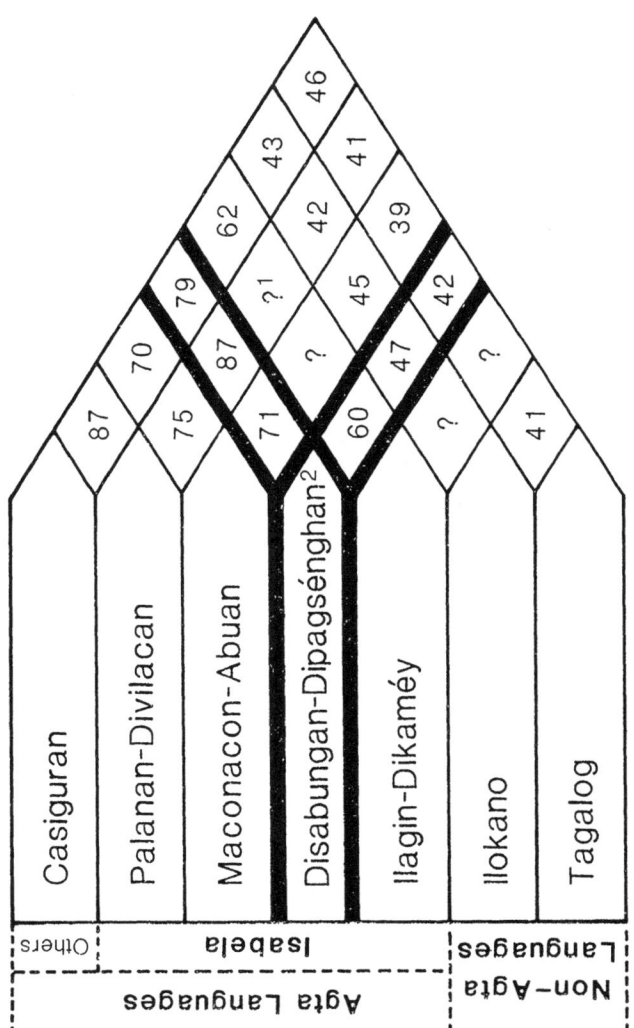

Data compiled and analyzed by Thomas Headland and Navin Rai.

[1]Not calculated.
[2]The study group.

178　　Living in a Lean-to

APPENDIX 4
Terms of Reference Among the Disabungan Agta

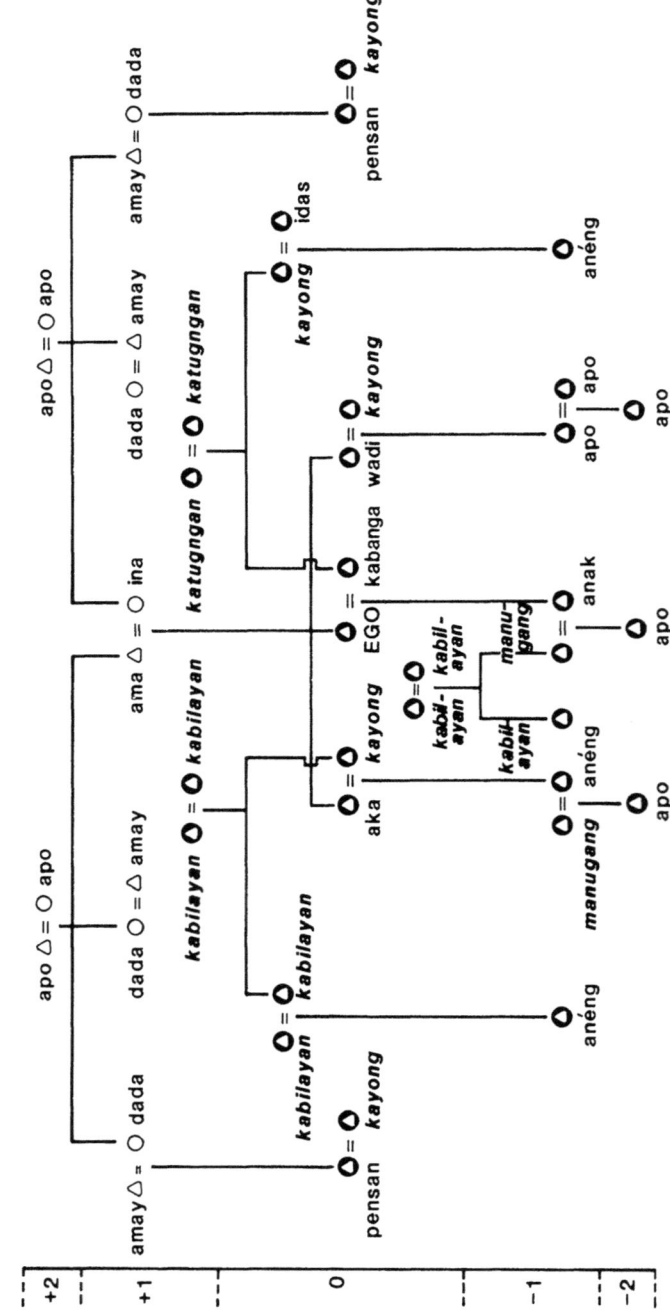

The non-italicized terms designate ego's kindred; the italicized, ego's affines. Symbols: △ male; ○ female; ◉ male or female

APPENDIX 5
Work/Non-Work Ratio among a Band of Disabungan Agta (per Economically Active Person per Day)[a]

Observation Group		Computed Daily Average[b]		Adjusted Daily Average[c]		Adjusted Ratio
Sex	Marital Status	% Work	% Non-work	% Work	% Non-work	Work Hrs.:Non-work Hrs.
Male	unmarried	23.0	77.0	11.1	88.9	1:8.02
	married	35.1	64.9	21.1	78.9	1:3.73
	average[d]	32.2	67.8	18.9	81.1	1:4.29
Female	unmarried	21.6	78.4	9.9	90.1	1:9.08
	married	15.6	84.4	5.1	94.9	1:18.67
	average	17.3	82.7	6.5	93.5	1:14.38
Agta average		23.9	76.1	12.1	87.9	1:7.26

[a]451 person-days of work observed.
[b]See Chapter Note 6.1 for definition of working time.
[c]Based on the observation that approximately one-third of working time is spent in leisure, "adjusted work" is calculated by subtracting 33% from "computed work."
[d]Entire available work force (aged 9 and above) of the band.

APPENDIX 6
Work Activity Schedule among a Band of Disabungan Agta (per Economically Active Person per Activity)[a]

Observation Group		Average Daily Work (Hrs.)	% of Work Time Per Activity					
Sex	Marital Status		Hunting	Gathering	Fishing	Trading	Swiddening	Other
Male	unmarried	5.52	74.2	2.2	9.2	2.6	1.1	10.7
	married	8.42	74.6	0.3	0.9	18.1	0.2	5.9
	average[b]	7.73	74.5	0.6	2.5	15.4	0.2	6.8
Female	unmarried	5.18	0.5	27.4	4.2	49.3	1.0	17.5
	married	3.74	13.2	22.9	7.0	23.6	1.5	31.8
	average	4.15	8.5	24.6	6.0	33.0	1.3	26.5
Agta average		5.74	48.0	10.3	3.8	22.5	0.7	14.8

[a] 2,593 person-hours of work observed.
[b] Entire available work force (aged 9 and above) of the band.

APPENDIX 7
Analysis of Hunting Activity of a Band of Disabungan Agta

		Number	%
PARTICIPANT			
	adult man	110	73.8
	adult woman	21	14.1
	young boy	18	12.1
NUMBER IN HUNTING PARTY			
	1	10	20.8
	2	16	33.4
	3	6	12.5
	4 or more	16	33.4
TOOL			
	shotgun	66	44.3
	bow and arrow	60	40.3
	machete	5	3.4
	none	18	12.0
TECHNIQUE			
	collective	14	27.4
	individual (daytime)	30	58.8
	individual (nighttime)	7	13.7
HUNTING GROUND			
	outside 3 km of swidden	37	77.1
	inside 3 km of swidden	11	22.9
GAME KILLED			
	wild pig	21	60.0
	deer	9	25.7
	monkey	5	14.3
CONSUMPTION vs. TRADE			
	wild pig		
	consumed (kg)	305	58.4
	traded (kg)	217	41.6
	deer		
	consumed (kg)	56	24.7
	traded (kg)	171	75.3
TRADE PARTNER			
	permanent agriculturalists	5	26.3
	mercantile groups	14	73.7

Total days of observation = 64
Total days of hunting = 53
Total hours of hunting = 3,805
Total hunting trips = 48

APPENDIX 8
Height and Weight of Agta Adults

Agta group	Average Height[a]		Average Weight[b]		Source
	Male	Female	Male	Female	
Palanan	5'1"	4'7"	95	96	M. Hanna (field notes)
Casiguran	5'1"	4'7"	90	75	Vanoverbergh (See Wastl 1957: 806–7)
Casiguran	5'2"	4'8"	102	84	Headland (1981a:4)
AVERAGE	5'1"	4'7"	96	85	

[a] In feet and inches.
[b] In pounds.

APPENDIX 9
Food Energy Conversion Table (per 100 g Raw Food)[a]

Food Item[b]	Food Energy (Cal)	Protein (g)	Fat (g)	Carbohydrates (g)
Wild pig meat	307.0	12.2	28.3	0.0
Deer meat	94.0	21.9	0.1	0.0
Monkey meat	200.5	17.1	14.2	0.0
Fish (*kulapia*)	112.5	17.5	4.1	0.0
Eel	95.0	17.5	2.3	0.0
Fresh water shrimp	83.0	16.6	1.3	0.0
Shellfish	97.0	9.4	0.8	12.2
Small crab	126.0	13.8	3.8	8.1
Wild yam (*ilus*)	103.0	1.9	0.1	25.2
Wild yam (*balo*)	112.0	1.2	0.0	28.3
Caryota palm	316.0	0.5	0.0	88.2
Honey	304.0	0.3	0.0	82.3
Fern shoot	37.0	3.8	2.1	2.9
Palm/rattan shoot	27.0	2.0	0.7	4.5
Guava	124.0	1.0	0.4	32.5
Palm/rattan fruit	79.0	0.6	1.2	18.6
Citrus fruit	59.0	0.5	0.3	15.3
Wild banana	90.0	1.3	0.3	23.2
Rice (undermilled)	362.0	8.5	2.0	76.9
Corn	386.0	8.8	4.3	80.9
Cassava	141.0	0.7	0.1	34.3
Sweet potato	136.0	1.1	0.4	32.3
Squash	34.0	1.9	0.4	7.3
Eggplant	24.0	1.0	0.2	5.7
Sugar cane	44.0	0.1	0.2	11.9
Sardine (canned)	202.0	19.2	13.3	0.3
Coffee (powder)	357.0	17.8	1.3	68.6
Sugar	346.0	2.2	0.2	83.9
Cracker biscuit	481.0	7.5	19.4	69.0
Liquor (distilled)	37.0	0.2	0.3	7.4

[a] Based on the food composition data provided by the Food and Nutrition Research Institute, Manila (see FNRI 1968).
[b] Food items consumed by the Disabungan Agta.

APPENDIX 10
Caloric Contribution of Activities[a]

Family	Contribution (in Kilocalories and Percentage)					
	Hunting	Gathering	Fishing	Trade	Swiddening	Total
I	74,919.3	46,135.3	2,340.0	158,850.2	18,512.0	300,756.8
	24.8%	15.3%	0.8%	52.8%	6.2%	100%
II	71,347.4	67,628.0	3,887.8	171,884.4	12,220.0	326,967.6
	21.7%	20.9%	1.2%	52.6%	3.7%	100%
III	68,055.8	37,059.5	5,552.0	141,682.4	15,023.0	267,372.7
	25.4%	13.9%	2.1%	53.0%	5.6%	100%
IV	68,226.0	52,888.0	7,842.0	212,147.6	9,391.0	350,534.6
	19.7%	15.1%	2.2%	60.5%	2.6%	100%
AVERAGE	282,548.5	203,710.8	19,621.0	684,564.6	55,146.0	1,245,631.0
	22.6%	16.4%	1.6%	55.0%	4.4%	100%

[a]This analysis is based on actual weighing of food procured by a band of Disabungan Agta. It was weighed in its fresh, raw and uncooked form before every meal for a period of four weeks during September and October. This analysis excludes minor items consumed in the camp and all items consumed outside the camp.

APPENDIX 11
Nutritional Intake of a Band of Disabungan Agta

Family	Food Energy (Cal)	Protein (g)	Fat (g)	Carbohydrate (g)
I	2,018.5	68.4	50.5	320.5
II	2,069.4	67.7	50.8	327.2
III	2,072.7	73.2	56.7	322.0
IV[a]	2,163.8	71.3	53.0	361.2
AVERAGE	2,081.1	70.2	52.8	332.7

These numbers represent intake per person per day. They were calculated by dividing the total energy, protein, etc., intakes of the family by the number of family members.

[a]During the period of data collection, I cooked and ate with Family IV; I imported outside rice and contributed it as my share to the family cooking. This contribution accounts for the higher food energy and carbohydrate intakes of Family IV.

APPENDIX 12
Energy Expenditure Among a Band of Disabungan Agta (per Adult per Day)

		Expenditure in Kilocalories (Hours)						
Sex	Period	Running	Swimming	Walking	Standing	Sitting	Lying	Sleeping	Total
Male	work	168.0[a] (0.2)[b]	—	450.8 (2.3)	130.9 (1.1)	105.0 (1.5)	—	—	854.7 (5.1)
	non-work	—	98.0 (0.2)	176.4 (0.9)	107.1 (0.9)	385.0 (5.5)	106.4 (1.9)	465.5 (9.5)	1,338.4 (18.9)
	TOTAL								2,193.1 (24.0)
Female	work	—	—	85.7 (0.4)	37.5 (0.3)	29.4 (0.5)	—	—	152.6 (1.2)
	non-work	—	96.6 (0.2)	191.5 (1.1)	116.3 (1.1)	465.0 (7.8)	109.4 (2.3)	430.9 (10.3)	1,409.7 (22.8)
	TOTAL								1,562.3 (24.0)

[a] Energy expenditure (given in kilcalories) is calculated from the estimated duration of activity, the body surface area (male = 1.4 and female = 1.2; see Appendix 8 and the nomogram provided by Schottelius and Schottelius [1978:481]), and Cal/m²/hr expenditure figures provided by Knoebel (1976:675).
[b] The estimated duration of the activity (given in hours) is derived from the work/non-work ratio for each sex (see Appendix 5). My own observations were used to verify the accuracy of the times used.

www.ingramcontent.com/pod-product-compliance
Lightning Source LLC
Jackson TN
JSHW070313120426
100741JS00007B/43